MW01061996

F

A Victorian Lady's Guide
to Fashion and Beauty

For my parents, Vickie and Eugene, who have always encouraged—and indulged—my love of beautiful things.

A Victorian Lady's Guide to Fashion and Beauty

Mimi Matthews

PEN & SWORD HISTORY

First published in Great Britain in 2018 by
PEN AND SWORD HISTORY
an imprint of
Pen and Sword Books Ltd
47 Church Street
Barnsley
South Yorkshire S70 2AS

Copyright © Mimi Matthews, 2018

ISBN 978 1 52670 504 4

The right of Mimi Matthews to be identified
as the author of this work has been asserted by her in accordance
with the Copyright, Designs and Patents Act 1988.

A CIP record for this book is available from the British Library
All rights reserved. No part of this book may be reproduced or
transmitted in any form or by any means, electronic or
mechanical including photocopying, recording or
by any information storage and retrieval system, without
permission from the Publisher in writing.

Printed and bound in India by Replika Press
by T J International, Padstow, Cornwall, PL28 8RW

Typeset in Times New Roman 10/12.5 by
Aura Technology and Software Services, India

Pen & Sword Books Ltd incorporates the imprints of Pen & Sword
Archaeology, Atlas, Aviation, Battleground, Discovery,
Family History, History, Maritime, Military, Naval, Politics, Railways,
Select, Social History, Transport, True Crime, Claymore Press,
Frontline Books, Leo Cooper, Praetorian Press, Remember When,
Seaforth Publishing and Wharncliffe.

For a complete list of Pen and Sword titles please contact
Pen and Sword Books Limited
47 Church Street, Barnsley, South Yorkshire, S70 2AS, England
E-mail: enquiries@pen-and-sword.co.uk
Website: www.pen-and-sword.co.uk

Contents

Acknowledgments

While researching and writing this book, I was privileged to have a great deal of support from friends, family, and professional peers. To them, I extend my heartfelt thanks.

Thanks are also due to the wonderful team at Pen and Sword Books; to Jon Wright for supporting this book from its inception; to Carol Trow for her patience, sensitivity, and general editing brilliance; to Laura Hirst for her kindness and attention to detail; to Jon Wilkinson for creating such a beautiful book cover; and to Mei Trow for giving so generously of his valuable time.

A very special thank you to the countless museums, universities, and archives that assisted in my research. I am particularly grateful to the Metropolitan Museum of Art, Wellcome Library, the Tokyo Fuji Art Museum, and the Musée de la Ville de Paris, Musée du Petit-Palais for the use of their illustrations, fashion plates, and paintings.

And finally, to Ash, Stella, Sapphire, Marzipan, and Centelleo, who have trudged along with me through good fashion days and bad. None of this would mean anything without you.

Mimi Matthews
January 2018

Introduction

Queen Victoria ascended the British throne in 1837. During the more than sixty years of her reign, women's fashion evolved from the restrictive, Gothic severity that exemplified the sheltered Victorian lady to the shirtwaists and no-nonsense tailor-made suits that would come to epitomize the turn of the century New Woman. In between, there were flounced skirts over wire cage crinolines, richly trimmed fabrics drawn back over bustles, and waistlines nipped to mere inches by steam-moulded corsets—silhouettes that are easily recognizable today from televised costume dramas, period movies, and Steampunk fairs and festivals.

As fashion was evolving, so too were trends in women's beauty. An era which began by prizing natural, bare-faced beauty ended with women purchasing cosmetics, such as lip rouge, synthetic perfumes, and chemical lighteners for their skin. By 1901, chemists were marketing beauty products to the masses, allowing for women of every age and every class to indulge in the latest hair and make-up trends.

Changes in fashion and beauty were spurred on by social and technological advancement. As women gained independence, clothing adapted to suit their newfound freedom. Unwieldy crinolines and bustles made way for dresses in which a lady could easily walk to work, ride her bicycle, or participate in sports such as golf and tennis. At the same time, the invention of the sewing machine and the discovery of aniline dyes further democratized fashion, making stylish silhouettes and vibrant colours available to a much wider range of women.

Victorian women's fashion and beauty is the primary focus of this book. However, rather than address the minute details of fabric density or the exact method for cutting a bodice or sewing a sleeve, I have chosen to give a broad overview of the changes in fashionable clothing, hairstyles, and cosmetics that took place from the advent of the era to the end of the nineteenth century. I have also included relevant historical events to put these changes into greater context. The result is what I hope will be a comprehensive—and comprehensible—survey of Victorian fashion and beauty, suitable for laypersons and historians alike. I hope you find it as enjoyable to read as I have to research and write.

PART I

Fashion

Chapter 1

The 1840s

'Although the present styles of toilette partake of the purest elegance, they are divested of all unnecessary and gorgeous decorations.'
Blackwood's Lady's Magazine, 1843.

The 1840s ushered in a decade of women's gowns designed in what some nineteenth century historians describe as the 'Victorian Gothic' style.[1] Gone were the sloping shoulders and enormous gigot sleeves (also known as leg-o'-mutton sleeves) which characterized the romantic silhouettes of the late 1820s and early to mid-1830s. In their place were pointed bodices, dome-shaped skirts, and long, tight sleeves which made it impossible for a lady to raise her arms above her head.

These were fashions designed for women who were expected to be dependent on those around them. Though a young and eventually transformative queen had ascended the British throne in 1837, ordinary women of the 1840s had very little freedom of their own. They were constrained not only by their clothing, but by the suffocating rules of society. This was especially true for those ladies of the middle and upper classes. For most of them, marriage and children were the ultimate goal. Work outside the home was discouraged, as was participation in competitive sports like golf or tennis.

Instead, women engaged in more restrained and ladylike pursuits such as needlework, painting, or playing the piano. They wrote letters, volunteered for charitable causes, and went shopping or for walks. Those women who wished for more strenuous exercise—and had the means to afford it—could also go horseback riding, garbed in riding costumes that were as restrictive and cumbersome as the rest of their clothing.

The 1840s Silhouette

At the beginning of the decade, women's dresses were angular and severe. Gowns were set low on the shoulder with sleeves worn long and tight to the arm. Some sleeves of this type featured a small frill, cap-piece, or puff near the shoulder. The bishop style of sleeve was also considered quite fashionable. It was pleated at the shoulder and became fuller as it extended down to the wrist where it was gathered into a cuff.

Dresses of the early 1840s had low set shoulders and long, tight-fitting sleeves. (*Women's Morning and Dinner Dresses*, 1840. Thomas J. Watson Library, Metropolitan Museum of Art.)

Bodices of the 1840s were long and tight-fitting, coming to a distinct point at the waist. They generally fastened at the back with buttons, laces, or hooks, making it difficult for a lady to dress and undress without assistance. In ladies' magazine of the day, a bodice was often referred to as a *corsage*. At the time, it was an accepted practice to call various elements of a woman's dress by the French name. Thus, a bodice became a *corsage*, a waistcoat became a *gilet*, and heart-shaped necklines were described as being cut *en coeur* or 'of the heart'.[2]

Some bodices had loosely folded, ruched, or plaited fabric down the front in a fan or V-shape. Others were accented with a ribbon sash or a narrow belt made of velvet. An 1842 edition of *Godey's Lady's Book* reports that velvet belts were generally 'of a darker tint than the dress' and were secured in front with either a loop-bow, a brooch, or 'a small elegant buckle'.

Skirts were fairly plain, but as the decade progressed they began to grow larger. Much of their increase in size was owed to a new method of setting the skirts, called gauging. An 1841 edition of the *Ladies' Cabinet of Fashion, Music, and Romance* claims that gauging was 'highly advantageous to the shape.' It consisted of:

> *'The top of the skirt, not quite half a quarter in depth, being gauged so as to sit flat round the hips; this mode of confining the excessive fullness of the skirt, at once displays and forms the shape in much more graceful manner than the present mode of setting it on.'*

To accommodate the fuller style of skirt, a bustle was introduced. Unlike the more dramatic wire cage bustles of the late Victorian era, the 1840s bustle was simply a padding of wool. This bustle pad was tied on round the waist and placed on the back of the hips, serving to give large skirts an even more pronounced dome-shape.

Another innovation of the early 1840s was the dress with two interchangeable bodices. This allowed a lady to have one bodice for daywear and one for eveningwear. Evening bodices were more revealing than day bodices. They were generally cut wide and low off the shoulder. For modesty, many ladies chose to cover the exposed portion of their skin with a lace bertha collar. A bertha was a wide, flat, round collar that covered the neck and shoulders. Berthas were also worn with day dresses and could be made of the same material as a woman's gown.

In evening dress, sleeves were short or elbow-length. For daywear, short sleeves were fairly uncommon until 1842 when, as the *Court, Lady's Magazine, Monthly Critic and Museum* reports:

> *'We have decidedly triumphed over our natural antipathy to short sleeves, for we wear them at all times now … although there is not much sublimity in either short or long sleeves, yet after the long war, that we waged against the former, except in ball costume it seems rather ridiculous to see them so generally.'*

Ball dresses of the early 1840s were made of crepe, tulle, or organdie, with under-skirts of silk or satin. The 1841 edition of the *Ladies' Cabinet of Fashion, Music, and Romance* reports:

> *'Those that we have seen had the corsages pointed at bottom, cut low, and draped round the top. The sleeves were very short, and either terminated by bouillons or ruches, and the skirt raised at the right side in front, and at the left at the back by a knot of ribbon or a gold agraffe.'*

Gauging at the waist resulted in fuller, dome-shaped skirts. (*La Mode*, July 1846. Thomas J. Watson Library, Metropolitan Museum of Art)

Though light fabrics like crepe and organdie remained fashionable for ball gowns, it was in the 1840s that the rich, heavy fabrics that we now associate with the Victorian era were beginning to come into fashion. According to an 1843 edition of *Godey's Lady's Book*, new materials for dresses included:

> '*Silks with a very narrow satin stripe – shaded or changeable satins – double levantines – or thick twilled silks – Scotch plaid velvets – oriental velvets – gros de Tours – embroidered India muslins – and very rich white Thibets damasked with satin flowers.*'

The use of luxurious fabrics even extended to those dresses worn for lounging around at home. For example, the 1844 edition of *Godey's Lady's Book* includes a fashion plate depicting a morning dress made of white cashmere 'trimmed with a facing of pink' and worn with a 'cap of light spotted lace, decorated with roses.'

By the mid-1840s, the Gothic silhouette was at last beginning to soften. The focus of women's fashion shifted downward toward the skirts where the voluminous fabric was embellished with elaborate trimmings, including lace, fringe, flounces, scallops, frogging, and ornamental buttons and bows. Meanwhile, rounded waists were gradually becoming more acceptable, though pointed waists still prevailed in the most fashionable gowns.

For eveningwear, necklines were low, sleeves were short, and skirts were often trimmed with lace and flowers. (*La Mode*, 1847. Thomas J. Watson Library, Metropolitan Museum of Art)

For eveningwear, necklines were low and cut either straight across or *en coeur*, with a slight dip at the centre. Sleeves were short and, along with necklines, were often trimmed with lace or tulle. At the same time, skirts were becoming increasingly elaborate. An 1846 edition of the *New Monthly Belle Assemblée* describes the current styles in skirts for evening dress, stating:

> *'Some satin robes, made with double skirts, have the upper one trimmed with lace. Some of the most novel of these dresses have the lace very broad, and looped on one side by a bouquet of flowers, or an ornament of jewelry.'*

This did not mean that plain dresses had fallen out of favour. For daywear, simpler gowns with subdued flounces and trimmings were still quite popular. They were also much more affordable since the cost of trimmings – such as lace, ribbons, and fringe – could add up to a tidy sum.

As the decade came to a close, long, tight sleeves began to loosen into a funnel or bell shape, foreshadowing the much larger pagoda sleeves that would appear in the 1850s. Skirts, which had become markedly fuller with each passing year, now required so much fabric that the material could no longer be gauged to the waist. Instead, it was once again pleated and gathered.

The overall silhouette was a far cry from the romantic 1830s, but the angular severity of the Victorian Gothic gown was at last showing glimpses – especially in the sleeves and the skirts – of what women's fashion would bring in the coming decades.

Undergarments: Corsets and Petticoats

The severe silhouette of the 1840s owed much to sturdy undergarments. These generally included a loose, knee-length cotton or linen chemise with short sleeves, a pair of cotton or linen drawers, a corset and corset cover, a bustle pad and several stiffened petticoats. The corset and petticoats were, perhaps, the most significant of these undergarments in terms of creating an 1840s shape. Without them, a woman could never hope to achieve the pronounced, hourglass figure so coveted in fashion of the time.

Corsets of the 1840s were gradually evolving from the longline, corded stays with shoulder straps that many ladies wore in the early nineteenth century to the shorter, more waist-constricting corsets worn by women in the 1850s and 1860s. Unlike the earlier stays, these corsets were often strapless and extended from the bosom to the hip. They were typically made of boned cotton or silk with laces in the back and a busk made of wood, whalebone, or steel inserted down the centre front to provide additional support.

As the century progressed, the wooden or whalebone busk at the front of the corset was replaced with a divided busk of steel which was set with a row of hooks and eyes. This allowed ladies a modicum of independence. They could now take their corset on and off without calling for the assistance of a maid or helpful family member.

Petticoats of the 1840s were another invaluable underpinning. Some were decorative satin, crepe, or tulle, made to be seen when an overskirt was drawn up or back. Others were strictly for shape and support. These were usually made of starched cotton or linen and could be quilted or corded to provide additional structure. Some stiffened petticoats were made out of horsehair and linen. These were called crinolines after the French words for horsehair (*crin*) and linen (*lin*). Crinolines would remain a popular—and sometimes controversial—undergarment for many decades to come.

Millinery: Poke Bonnets, Capotes, and Lace Matron's Caps

A Victorian lady never ventured outdoors without first putting on her bonnet. In the 1840s, poke bonnets were quite fashionable. Designed with a small crown and a wide, rounded brim that projected forward over the face, poke bonnets were often made of straw and trimmed with crepe, gauze, silk ribbons, feathers, or flowers. A soft-crowned style of bonnet, known as the capote, was also very much in fashion. Capotes were low and close fitting with rigid, round brims. They could be made from a range of materials, including straw, crepe, and velvet, and were frequently trimmed with lace, gauze, feathers, and flowers. In addition to trimmings on the outside, both poke bonnets and capotes were also sometimes trimmed on the interior brim with quilled lace, tulle, or small tufts of flowers.

When at home, Victorian matrons and spinsters donned caps made of delicate lace, fine muslin, or knit or crocheted cotton. Some caps had long lappets falling down on either side. Some were ornamented with ribbons or flowers. For December of 1846, the *New Monthly Belle Assemblée* reports:

> *'The prettiest caps for very youthful matrons are of a very small size; they are composed of rows of blond or lace, each divided by a very small wreath of red clematis: this style of garniture has the effect of the hair being strewed with flowers.'*

Unmarried young ladies were discouraged from wearing lace caps indoors. However, if they were over the age of twenty-seven and still unwed, they were considered to have entered the realm of spinsterhood, thus making a demure lace cap appropriate for indoor wear.

Footwear: Silk Stockings and Congress Boots

Victorian ladies always wore stockings with their gowns. An 1847 edition of *Godey's Lady's Book* declares that 'the best stockings for general wear are those made of lamb's wool, vigonia and Shetland knit'. For women who were not very active and, thus, less inclined to sweat, *Godey's* recommended silk stockings, calling them 'the most elegant of all coverings for the feet' and 'far more comfortable than either cotton or linen'. Stockings were rolled onto the leg and secured above the knee with garters. Black was a common shade for both day and eveningwear; however, stockings came in a variety of colours such as brown, white, grey, and blue.

The style of shoes that an 1840s lady wore depended on the occasion. For instance, when out walking or visiting the shops, she might don a sensible pair of double-soled ankle boots made of goat, kid, or calfskin. Ladies' boots could also be made in more delicate textures such as kerseymere, cashmere, silk, or satin. In the late 1840s, the 'Congress Boot,' made with an elastic gore, was popular in both the United States and the United Kingdom. Congress Boots were deemed indispensable for walking. They earned the patronage of Queen Victoria and fashion magazines of the day claimed that the queen often wore them herself while on her daily rambles.

For more formal occasions such as a dinner party, a dance, or a ball, ladies of the 1840s wore slippers, ribbon sandals, or white satin evening boots. Slippers were generally flat with a box-shaped toe. Toward the end of the decade, a very small heel was added.

The Congress Boot was popular in both the United States and the United Kingdom. (Shoe Shopping, The Congress Boot. *Godey's Lady's Book*, 1848)

Outerwear: Cloaks and Mantelets

For brisk mornings, chilly carriage rides, or cold winter walks, most ladies of the 1840s donned a warm cloak. Fashionable cloaks of the period generally fell several inches shorter than the hem of a lady's skirts. They came in a variety of styles. There were mantle cloaks, which draped loosely over the arms and shoulders; fitted cloaks with long Persian sleeves; and cloaks with capes which vaguely resembled those on a gentleman's greatcoat.

An 1842 day dress worn with a mantle and an evening dress worn with a pair of black net mitts. (Thomas J. Watson Library, Metropolitan Museum of Art)

The 1841 edition of the *Ladies' Cabinet of Fashion* describes stylish cloaks of green satin 'spotted with crimson velvet, and lined with crimson satin'. Cloaks of black or dark-coloured velvet were also considered to be quite fashionable, as were cloaks made of wool or *cashmere de barege*. According to the 1842 edition of the *Ladies' Cabinet of Fashion*:

> *'Some are composed of velvet embroidered all around in a rich fancy border, with coloured silks. Some are lined with satin, others with gros de Naples. The cloak is always of a black or dark colour, and the lining a striking contrast being either rose, groiselle, or maize.'*

For spring and summer, cloaks were usually too heavy. Instead, many ladies chose to wear a mantelet. A mantelet was essentially a short, loose cloak with either wide sleeves or long ends which fell down the front of a lady's dress. They were made of light-coloured silks, embroidered muslins, or rich satins bordered with patterns in relief.

Accessories: Gloves and Mittens

During the Victorian era, gloves were a fashionable necessity. Whether walking, shopping, or waltzing at a society ball, the rules of etiquette simply did not permit a well-bred lady to go about with uncovered hands. As a result, there were gloves made for every conceivable occasion and every possible activity. There were long gloves, demi-long gloves, short gloves, and fingerless mittens or mitts.

For daywear, ladies of the 1840s generally donned short gloves. These could be made of silk, cloth, or kidskin. Some gloves and mitts had velvet cuffs. Others featured decorative embroidery or trim. According to the 1841 edition of *Blackwood's Lady's Magazine*:

> *'The prettiest gloves are embroidered in silk and gold, and the opening fastened with a silk cord, with a ruche of thread lace round the top.'*

For evening, many ladies of the 1840s wore gloves or mittens made of black filet. Filet was a variety of silk net or lace with a square, openwork pattern. The 1840 edition of *Godey's Lady's Book* reports:

> *'Long and short gloves and mittens, of black filet, are universally adopted. They are trimmed at the tops or round the wrists with narrow black lace.'*

Evening gloves of white silk net or white kid trimmed with satin ribbon were also quite popular, as were gloves trimmed with flowers, feathers, or silver or gold cord.

Jewellery: Chatelaines, Bracelets, and Belt Buckles

In keeping with the Gothic style of women's dress, jewellery of the 1840s was fairly restrained. Even so, there were several pieces which found favour with fashionable ladies. One of these was the chatelaine. A chatelaine consisted of a small ring attached to a watch chain on which were fastened a cluster of tiny ornaments, both decorative and practical. There were seals, rings, scissors, miniature fans, and other miniscule charms of silver, gold, mother-of-pearl, or coral. The chatelaine was worn suspended from the waist in the same manner which a medieval lady might carry the household keys.

Bracelets were another popular item of jewellery during the 1840s. They were often made of gold and worn one on each wrist or several on the same arm. However, according to the 1842 edition of the *Court Magazine and Monthly Critic*, the most fashionable ladies wore only 'a single gold bracelet on the right arm above the glove.'

Some of the most common items of jewellery during the 1840s were the small, elegant buckles which ladies used to secure their fashionable belts. They could be made of gold or silver and were sometimes enamelled or set with jewels. The 1848 edition of *Godey's Lady's Book* reports:

'A silver or pearl buckle is preferable, as it will harmonize with almost any style of dress: some very elegant ones in enamel and set with brilliants, have been seen.'

Chapter 2

The 1850s

'Let us hope that serious measures will soon be adopted for moderating the extent of crinoline, or the consequences may be very grave.'
                                        The *Ladies' Companion,* 1855.

The 1850s was a decade of bright colours, exotic fabrics, and womanly curves. Gone were the restrictive Gothic gowns of the 1840s. In their place were distinctively feminine frocks with flowing, pagoda-style sleeves and impossibly full skirts supported by the newly introduced wire cage crinoline. This was a decade during which women's fashion was influenced by the Crimean War, the emergence of the modern sewing machine, and the increasing independence of women themselves. No longer content to be mere drawing room ornaments, ladies of the 1850s were beginning to break free from their domestic prisons and demand their rights in the outside world.

This was also the decade which marked the beginning of the Second Empire in France, a period which lasted from 1852-1870. After staging a bloodless coup in December of 1851, Louis-Napoleon Bonaparte, then president of the Second French Republic, was crowned Napoleon III, Emperor of France. As his Empress, he chose the young, Spanish-born beauty, Eugénie de Montijo, 16th Countess of Teba and 15th Marquise of Ardales. They were married in January of 1853, launching both Eugénie's reign as Empress of France and her reign as the ultimate arbiter of fashionable dress in Europe, Britain, and even America.

The 1850s Silhouette

At the beginning of the decade, the basic shape of women's gowns had changed little from the late 1840s. The silhouette was distinctly hourglass with small, tight-fitting waists and dome-shaped skirts which continued to grow ever larger. Rich fabrics were still all the rage and, according to the 1850 edition of the *New Belle Assemblée*, velvet was 'far more in vogue' than silk.

For daywear, two and three-piece ensembles consisting of a jacket-like bodice, a waistcoat, and a skirt were very much in fashion. Some jacket bodices extended down to flare over the hips. These were called *basque* bodices or *basque* waists,

A yellow ball gown (right) and a day dress paired with a fashionable cashmere shawl. (*Le Moniteur de la Mode*, 1850. Thomas J. Watson Library, Metropolitan Museum of Art)

a style that was particularly popular in the 1850s. Waistcoats, sometimes referred to as *gilets*, were also very popular, leading an 1852 edition of the *London and Paris Ladies' Magazine of Fashion* to declare:

> *'Waistcoats have found too many admirers not to belong in fashion under every variety of dress, in colour as well as material. We have seen them even in lace and embroidered muslin.'*

Pagoda sleeves were fashionable throughout the decade. They were narrow at the armhole but grew substantially wider as they reached the elbows and wrists. An 1882 edition of *Ward and Lock's Home Book* describes the pagoda sleeves of the 1850s as being 'copied from the Chinese, wide and open' and states that they had the added benefit of making a lady's hands 'appear smaller by contrast with the aperture from which they emerge.'

Pagoda sleeves were paired with false undersleeves made of white lace, muslin, or cambric. Also known as *engageantes*, they were tied, buttoned, or tacked into the armhole of the pagoda sleeve and could easily be taken out and tacked into the sleeves of a different gown or removed from the sleeve altogether for laundering. Undersleeves of the 1850s often featured decorative cuffs trimmed with fine lace or embroidery. As an 1851 edition of the *Ladies' Companion at Home and Abroad* reports:

> '*Under-sleeves are more in favour than ever in half-dress toilettes; they are trimmed for the most elegant ones with expensive lace, or else beautifully embroidered.*'

Though pagoda sleeves were quite popular, some gowns of the early 1850s continued to be made with sleeves that were long and fairly close fitting. These sleeves often featured decorative cuffs. The *London and Paris Ladies' Magazine of Fashion* reports that, in 1852, 'deep gauntlet cuffs, called mousquetaire' were very much in use. Inspired by the deep, wide cuffs worn by musketeers in the seventeenth and eighteenth centuries, cuffs à la mousquetaire opened at the side, forming a sharp point. They were particularly popular in day dresses and riding habits.

For eveningwear, Victorian ladies of the early 1850s wore dresses with low necklines and short sleeves trimmed in lace, tulle, or fringe. These sorts of trimmings were perennial favourites for ball gowns and evening dresses, but there were other innovations as well. For example, 1851 saw the introduction of a velvet ribbon stamped to look like lace. The 1851 issue of the *New Belle Assemblée* reports that such decadent trimmings were paired with equally decadent gowns, writing:

> '*Some of the most elegant are composed of velvet; ruby, green, and a bright shade of violet, are favourite hues … Some are trimmed with black lace, and a stamped velvet ribbon … Others are trimmed with passementerie, in imitation of embroidery in relief; these garnitures are equally novel and elegant. Ruches of ribbons, disposed in zigzag, are also employed, and so are flat fancy trimmings, but neither are so much in vogue as the two first garnitures I have mentioned.*'

The combination of jacket, waistcoat, and skirt that had taken daytime fashion by storm was also seen in eveningwear, but though elements of women's fashion may have been masculine in design, there was no mistaking the beauty and femininity of the flowing lines, rich fabrics, and colours. To that end, the May 1852 issue of *Godey's Lady's Book* reports on the increasing popularity of patterned silks in a variety of beautiful shades:

> *'The spring silks are principally of mode colors, striped, plaided, and waved. The stripes are sometimes of embroidery patterns, in different colors. India silks are in every variety, of beautiful shades, and will be very much worn as a neat and inexpensive dress. Pale violet, blue, green, and mode colors predominate. Their advantage is, that there is no up or down, right or wrong side, and will bear turning, and even washing in clear soapsuds.'*

By 1853, the waistcoat style had begun to give way to the eighteenth century inspired *caraco* or *caraco corsage*. The *caraco* was a loose, thigh length jacket with an open front that was usually worn over a chemisette. It first appeared on the Victorian fashion scene in 1848, but was not widely worn until the early to mid-1850s. Though it did not surpass the tight, *basque* bodice in popularity, for at home wear, the *caraco* was considered to be in far better taste. As the 1853 issue of the *Ladies' Companion and Monthly Magazine* explains:

> *'Some people, when at home, wear a tight-fitting corsage, with basques different from the skirt; but this is not considered in good taste; it is only with a caraco that this may be done, or with a corsage caraco; that is to say a corsage which is not tight to the shape, and which is trimmed with lace or fringe: the plainest are those with rows of velvet or galon.'*

The *caraco* was not the only throwback to the eighteenth century. The 1850s saw a general revival of eighteenth century styles. A profusion of lace and trimmings decorated day dresses which were made in even richer materials. Meanwhile, ball gowns became more extravagant. An 1854 edition of the *London and Paris Ladies' Magazine of Fashion* reports that fashionable organdie, tulle, and taffeta ball gowns of the season were made with double or triple skirts trimmed with lace, flowers, marabou feathers, or gold and silver embroidery. The upper skirts were often 'raised in drapery at each side by bunched flowers or bows of ribbon.'

October of 1853 marked the beginning of the Crimean War. This had a visible influence on British fashion, especially in terms of bold colours and rich trimmings. According to fashion historian Cecil Willett Cunnington:

> *'There was a distinct liking for "Oriental" effects and Turkish style in a host of details. The rich conglomeration of colours favoured in Eastern embroidery, with Turkish tassels, crescent brooches and ornaments, displayed our sympathy with our "gallant ally"— of the moment.'*

Day dresses with pagoda sleeves and engageantes. (*Magasin des Demoiselles*, 1855. Thomas J. Watson Library. Metropolitan Museum of Art)

Rich fabrics and colours were just as popular in the United States. In addition to silks, taffetas, and velvets, there was silk plush and cashmere. Meanwhile shades of deep green, dark olive, and *Sevres* blue only served to enhance the luxuriousness of gowns for both day and evening.

By the mid-1850s, there was little change in the overall silhouette of women's gowns except for in the ever-increasing size of the skirts. Inspired by the voluminous skirts worn by the Empress Eugénie, they were often trimmed with row upon row of stiff flounces and stood out from the body over layers of petticoats and heavy crinolines. Bodices remained tight to the shape and wide, pagoda sleeves with lace or cambric undersleeves continued to be fashionable in day dresses.

Many stylish Victorian ladies wore light-coloured skirts paired with a dark velvet jacket or *caraco*. Some of the jackets of this type featured sleeves which were slashed open from the shoulder to the wrist to expose the cambric undersleeve. The cuff of the sleeve was then turned up just enough to show the fall of the undersleeve at the wrist.

One of the most notable events of the 1850s – at least in terms of women's fashion – was the 1856 invention of the wire cage crinoline. Made of graduated hooped wires secured by fabric tape, this technological marvel could accommodate skirts that were fuller and heavier than ever before. As a result, during the years from 1856 through 1866, skirts grew to their largest proportions of the century. By the end of the 1850s, it sometimes took as much as eighteen yards of fabric to complete a gown.

As the decade came to a close, fashionable ensembles that converted from day to evening with the removal of a jacket or detachable bodice were very much in style. Day dresses frequently had a belted waist and bodices were typically buttoned all the way up to the neck. When it came to sleeves, the wide, pagoda style of the previous years was slowly trending toward a narrower bell-shaped or funnel style sleeve. Short sleeves continued to be preferred for evening dress and, though satin was making a comeback, silk was still the most common fabric for ball gowns. An 1859 edition of *Peterson's Magazine* reports:

> *'Rich silks of plain colors, poplins, and plaid silks and poplins of very light colors, are all fashionable. Velvet trimmings woven in the material are very much worn, and have a rich, massive appearance suited to the season. Granite or speckled silks in various shades of grey are also fashionable. These are trimmed with bright colors, such as cherry, bright blue, bright green, collar and cuffs or plaids.'*

A suitable coda to this fashionable decade is provided by the 1859 issue of *Godey's Lady's Book*. Pausing for a moment from their advice on stylish fabrics and colours, they address the new fashion in enormous skirts, writing:

> *'Generally speaking, young ladies are now presenting a very formidable appearance of amplitude ... We do not, by any means, then, ask our young ladies, in defiance of fashion and foolishness, to grow "beautifully less;" but we would suggest to them to let these expansions become intellectual as well as superficial. It surely would be ridiculous to carry a narrow mind and contracted heart under that monstrous outward show.'*

A fashionable ball gown with skirts festooned with roses. (*Journal des Demoiselles*, 1858. Thomas J. Watson Library, Metropolitan Museum of Art)

Undergarments: The Controversial Wire Cage Crinoline

The fashionable hourglass shape of the 1850s was conjured by a tiny, corseted waist and a wide, impractical profusion of skirts. The silhouette was both impossibly feminine and, considering the enormous size of the gowns, surprisingly dainty. To achieve it, one naturally needed a substantial corset. However, the primary component of the mid-Victorian shape was the crinoline.

A crinoline was essentially a petticoat, made of horsehair or some other stiffening material which held the skirts of a gown out from the body. The horsehair petticoat had been in use in England from as early as the 1820s. By the early 1850s, Victorian ladies were beginning to take note of the wide, voluminous skirts worn by the Empress Eugénie, wife of Napoleon the III of France. Eugénie was the undisputed leader of fashion in the mid-nineteenth century. She had a reputation for taste and elegance and it was to her that the fashionable world looked for guidance 'before adopting a new toilette or a fresh coiffure'.[4]

Eugénie's preference for wide skirts caused the rest of the fashionable female world to follow suit, thus setting off what is popularly known as the crinoline era. Soon, skirts had grown to such enormous proportions that the horsehair petticoat was often not strong enough to support them. As a result, ladies were forced to wear several layers of very heavy petticoats or crinolines in order to achieve the desired effect. This was far from ideal.

Fortunately, the difficulty was remedied by the 1856 invention of the wire cage crinoline. With its strong but lightweight hooped wires and fabric tape, it allowed skirts to expand to their largest size yet. An unforeseen benefit of this was that ladies of the era no longer had to resort to tight lacing of their corsets to achieve the hourglass silhouette. In proportion to skirts of this magnitude their waists inevitably appeared smaller by comparison.

This benefit was likely offset by the limitations imposed by the size of a lady's skirts. Not only did the crinoline make a lady wider and less mobile than she had been in previous decades, it also impacted the lives of everyone in her wake—as evidenced by countless articles, pamphlets, cartoons, and even a one act crinoline play of the era. According to the anonymous author of the 1858 one penny pamphlet *The Dangers of Crinoline, Steel Hoops, &c*:

> 'No one can deny that an evil of the greatest magnitude has for some time been making serious inroads into the health, morals, and happiness of this country, in the shape of an absurd and preposterous fashion, dignified with the incomprehensible designation of CRINOLINE. This monstrous innovation, like a restless spectre, invades the domestic hearth, and stalks abroad in the streets, a gaunt and grisly phantom, whose "bones are marrowless."'

The author goes on to address (in the same melodramatic language) the pervasiveness of the crinoline in Victorian society:

> 'Old women tottering on the verge of the grave, enshrine their decrepit bones within it; young children, not long released from the trammels of swaddling clothes, jerk their little forms about in it; ugly women, pretty women, dark women, fair women, are all under the diabolical influence of CRINOLINE.'

True to the title of the pamphlet, after ridiculing the appearance of short, fat women in crinolines, and tall, thin shapeless women in crinolines, the author begins to present the multitude of dangers associated with the wearing of this 'scaffolding' of wire and horse-hair 'with puffs inserted, and, at intervals, hoops of steel or cane'. The dangers range from rheumatism, cold, and colic caused by the 'cold currents' and 'clouds of dust' that blow up the wide skirts, to horrific accidents caused by the crinoline catching in doors, bursting into flames, or causing its wearer to be blown off a cliff.

Amongst these heartrending tales, is the story of a 'beautiful maiden' in 1857 Yorkshire who went for a walk with her sweetheart whilst wearing a crinoline made of steel hoops. A thunderstorm was brewing and, predictably, the young lady's metal crinoline attracted a bolt of lightning, which struck her and nearly killed her. She awoke many days later vowing to never wear crinolines again.

Another gruesome tale, aptly titled *Shocking Case of a Lady of Title being nearly Burnt to Death*, relates the story of Lady B__, 'the acknowledged queen of fashion'. Whilst warming herself near the fire at a high society party, Lady B__'s skirts briefly brushed into the flames and she went up like the proverbial torch.

A woman wearing a wire cage crinoline is blown off a cliff. (*The Dangers of Crinoline, Steel Hoops, &c.*, London: G. Vickers, 1858)

The burns on her face, hands, and body were so disfiguring and severe that Lady B__ refused to ever see any of her friends again. She withdrew completely from the world, living out the rest of her miserable days in a convent in Italy.

Sentiment against crinolines was strong – especially male sentiment. An 1883 publication, titled *The Great Anti-Crinoline League*, begins with the following quote from the *Pall Mall Gazette*:

> *'We can suggest nothing better than an Anti-Crinoline League of eligible men who should bind themselves by fearful oaths never to dance, drive, dine, or enter into any tenderer relation with any wearer of "stiffeners," "wires," or "whalebone," in whatsoever form.'*

And the 1866 tract, *The Glories of Crinoline*, is somewhat condescendingly dedicated:

> *'To Those Numberless Ladies throughout the civilized world who are wise enough to avoid extremes, and who prefer to be the possessor of a modest modicum of moderate charms rather than the bearers of an immodest mountain of immoderate monstrosities.'*

Even in newspapers, such as *The Illustrated News of the World*, men bemoaned the encroaching effect of the crinoline. It crowded them out of omnibuses, cabs, and carriages. It crowded them out of pews in church. And it even prevented them from enjoying their 'fair share' of the public sidewalk.

Meanwhile, despite the limitations of their skirts, women of the mid-nineteenth century were beginning to feel empowered. In 1857, the Married Women's Property Bill was first discussed in parliament. In 1858, *The English Women's Journal* was founded, followed in 1859 by the formation of The Society for Promoting the Employment of Women. Women's colleges were springing up all across Great Britain and Victorian ladies were concerning themselves not only with women's education and employment, but also with suffrage and the rights of wives. In the 1864 publication, *Crinoline in its Bissextile Phases*, a lady responds to the male demand that females give up their crinolines with a verse which speaks volumes for feminine feeling in the Victorian era:

> *'They tell us, again, in a bustling street*
> *Our Crinolines hurt their poor legs or feet.*
> *Not badly, I trust, — 'twere the doctor to pay,*
> *My recipe is, keep out of our way.'*

According to author Julie Wosk, fashion historians of the day called the invention of the wire cage crinoline 'the first great triumph of the machine age.' In her book *Women and the Machine*, Wosk goes on to state that the various satirical images that sprang up of ladies of the era in their wire crinolines revealed as much about the century's ambivalence toward new technologies as about their feelings toward frivolous female fashions. The public was equally ambivalent about the changing role of women in society. Their giant crinolines were, at face value, a silly conceit, however those very garments made women formidable and difficult to ignore.

Millinery: Leghorns, Drawn Bonnets, and Flower Crowns

By the early 1850s, modesty was no longer the primary concern when choosing a bonnet. Instead, bonnets were beginning to be seen as merely ornamental. Following the fashionable example of the Empress Eugénie, Victorian ladies began to wear their bonnets tipped further back on their heads, thus displaying more of their hair and face.

Some women took this style to an extreme, placing the bonnet so far back that it looked as if it might fall off. When the Empress Eugénie came to London on an Imperial visit in 1855, fashion writers of the day used the opportunity to instruct ladies on the proper placement of their tipped back bonnets. The 21 April 1855 edition of the *Morning Post* reports:

> *'Although the bonnet of the Empress Eugénie displays fully her face and hair, it does not convey to the beholder the idea of its being likely to fall from the head behind, but rather seems to cling to and support the hair in that position. This gives a lightness and grace of carriage to the head totally distinct from that boldness and barefacedness which have characterized the English adoption of the French Imperial fashion.'*

Victorian ladies of the 1850s often wore Leghorn or fancy straw bonnets trimmed with tulle, feathers, and velvet ribbons or wreathed with violets, ivy, lilies of the valley or hyacinths. Ears of wheat, bunches of berries, field flowers, and apple and apricot blossoms were also used as trimmings.

Some ladies of the 1850s wore silk bonnets that were trimmed in velvet or lace. Others wore drawn bonnets, made of silk that had been gathered or bunched into channels between rows of cane or wire. For evening dress, ladies wore crowns of flowers or headdresses composed of bands of lace or ribbon with trimmings of flowers, ribbon, or other decorative ornaments puffed over each ear. An 1852 edition of *Le Moniteur de la Mode* describes one such headdress that was fashionable that summer:

> *'Head-dress of taffeta ribbon. On each side, the ribbon is turned back on itself so as to form two loops; and it is ornamented with a moss rose and its buds surrounded with moss without foliage.'*

Footwear: Embroidery, Ribbons, and High Heels

In keeping with the luxurious fabrics and trimmings of the decade, fashionable shoes of the 1850s were embellished with expensive beads, lace, and ribbons. An 1853 edition of *Godey's Lady's Book* reports that the latest Parisian fashions in footwear included shoes worn with 'large bows of ribbon on the instep' and satin evening boots ornamented with glass bugles, while an 1851 edition of the *Ladies' Companion and Monthly Magazine* states that:

> *'Only Cinderella's slippers could be more exquisite than some we have just been shown, of the Duchess of S—th—rl—d's, in one pair of which the lilac's leaf and blossom make the fronts and backs, and are mingled in the rosette on the instep.'*

For evening, women's satin or canvas slippers embroidered with silken threads or glass beads were very fashionable, as were shoes made of embroidered kidskin or enamelled leather. According to the *Ladies' Companion and Monthly Magazine*:

> *'Nothing can exceed the beautiful appearance of gold or silver threads on coloured, white, or bronzed leather, or would be more in keeping with the present almost oriental magnificence of evening dress.'*

Meanwhile, as the *Ladies' Companion and Monthly Magazine* reports, an effort was underway to 'add an inch to the feminine stature by the addition of what are called military heels'. Heeled shoes were gradually accepted, but an 1857 issue of *Godey's Lady's Book* was quick to warn its readers that:

> *'Care should be taken that the heel be not high, for, if so, it entirely destroys the grace of the body by throwing it out of its perpendicular; and a lady, instead of becoming like a graceful pillar, resembles rather a leaning tower, and that most awkwardly so.'*

Outerwear: Mantles, Cloaks, and Cashmere Shawls

Fashionable outwear of the 1850s included a range of mantles and cloaks. There were knee-length mantles with shoulder capes and rich, silk cloaks trimmed with velvet or lace. According to the 1854 edition of *Peterson's Magazine*, the most fashionable cloaks were short in length and 'gathered or plaited' at the shoulders. One such style, made for eveningwear, is described as having 'a hood of black lace' and fastening at the throat with 'a bow of black velvet.'

A selection of
mantles from 1853.
(Thomas J. Watson
Library, Metropolitan
Museum of Art)

Shawls and wraps were another fashionable option in 1850s outerwear. Available in all weights of fabrics, they graced the shoulders of women in every stratum of society. Ladies of fashion favoured shawls of silk, lace, gauze, or muslin, but perhaps the most coveted shawls of all were the rich, cashmere shawls from India. They were costly and rare, which made them all the more desirable to the ladies of the Western world. According to an 1858 edition of the *Ladies' Companion and Monthly Magazine*:

'Even in Europe with their many beautiful imitations, the true Cashmere shawl is still sought, and paid for at enormous prices. Even in India it is by no means unusual for a rajah to pay ten thousand rupees (five thousand dollars) for one of the finest of these productions, and which, in all probability, will have cost the labour of a whole family for a lifetime.'

Cashmere (or Kashmir) shawls were made from the wool of goats in the Kashmir region of India. They were as warm as they were luxurious. During the early nineteenth century, they helped keep ladies from catching a chill in their thin, Empire gowns. As the century progressed and ladies' fashions evolved into heavy ensembles, layered with petticoats and crinolines, cashmere shawls continued to be as vitally important to fashionable women's dress as ever. In the 1850s, it was not uncommon to see ladies sporting enormous cashmere shawls which had been folded on the diagonal and were worn draped round their shoulders, descending in a large triangle all the way down the back of their skirts. Ladies also donned shawls at home, over their housedresses or even their nightgowns.

By the 1870s, the popularity of the cashmere shawl was on the decline. This had less to do with the dictates of fashion and more with global politics and famine. As Sir Walter Roper Lawrence relates in his 1895 book *The Valley of Kashmir*:

> *'The shawl industry is now unfortunately a tradition—a memory of the past. The trade received its deathblow when war broke out between Germany and France in 1870, and I have been told by an eye-witness of the intense excitement and interest with which the Kashmiri shawl-weavers watched the fate of France in that great struggle—bursting into tears and loud lamentations when the news of Germany's victories reached them.'*

Any lingering hopes of the cashmere shawl weaving industry being revived were dashed when famine visited the Valley of Kashmir in 1877-1879. According to Lawrence, none suffered so greatly during that famine than the poor shawl-weavers. This did not mean that shawls and wraps fell out of fashion. Whether made of gauze, silk, muslin, or lace, a well-draped shawl was still an integral part of women's fashions well into the twentieth century.

Accessories: Kid Gloves, Painted Fans, and Lace Parasols

Gloves and mittens continued to be worn throughout the 1850s. The 1852 edition of the *London and Paris Ladies' Magazine of Fashion* reports that the most popular gloves that year were made in 'a moderate length' with trimmings at the top to correspond with those on a lady's dress. For daywear, there were coloured gloves of French kid or Swedish leather. White gloves were only permissible for evening. When worn at a ball, they were generally made of silk, satin, or kid.

Painted fans were another fashionable accessory of the 1850s. Of these, the most stunning were those exhibited by M. Duvelleroy of Paris during the Great Exhibition of 1851. According to the *Illustrated Exhibitor*, these exquisitely crafted fans 'excited the admiration of all the ladies' who visited M. Duvelleroy's stall at the Crystal Palace in London. They were painted with elaborately detailed scenes of ladies and gentlemen, grand houses, and scenic landscapes—elegant images which made them the perfect accompaniment to a lady's luxurious evening dress or ball gown.

When outdoors, Victorian ladies employed a parasol to protect their complexions from the sun. Fashionable parasols were often covered in black or white lace. They also came in coloured silks with lace or fringe trim and handles made of carved ivory. During the 1850s, many young ladies fell into the odd habit of putting their parasol handles against—or even into—their mouths. In his 1855 book *Motley*, Cuthbert Bede addresses the 'odious feminine fashion of sucking parasol-handles,' enquiring of his female readers:

'Why do you do it, young ladies? Do you think it coquettish? Is it that the act itself gives you any pleasure? Is it that there is some mysterious Corsican-brother affinity between the ivory of the handle and the ivory of your teeth? Is it to impress upon the minds of dull young men that your lips love a certain amount of pressure? Is it to draw attention to the "Oh! ruddier-than-the-cherry" of your lips by the contrast afforded by the whiteness of the parasol-handle? Is it to convey an idea of "sweets to the sweet" that you thus assume the appearance of a child sucking "goodies"? If it is not for all or any of these reasons, why do you suck your parasol handles?'

Jewellery: Cabochon Bracelets, Cameo Brooches, and Venetian Gold Chains

There were many styles of jewellery that were fashionable during the 1850s. Ladies wore diamond bracelets set with opals, emeralds, or amethysts. Enamelled bracelets and brooches were also quite popular, as were those set with large, cabochon stones. Some fashionable ladies favoured brooches set with cameo portraits, brooches ornamented with precious stones, or brooches and pins shaped like insects, bows, or knots.

By the mid-1850s, lower necklines on ladies' dresses prompted a resurgence in the popularity of necklaces. These necklaces were often made of fine, Venetian gold chain from which was suspended a small jewelled cross or medallion. For eveningwear, many ladies wore a single row of brilliant-cut diamonds or simple strands of coral beads or pearls. For very young ladies, the 1855 edition of *Godey's Lady's Book* reports that 'a simple gold chain, the light Venetian link, with no pendant but a small medallion passing once around the neck' was imminently suitable. *Godey's* goes on to declare that:

'Nothing can be in more taste than a necklace on a thin, bony, or discolored neck. Very few women in our country should venture upon one after thirty.'

Victorian Dress Reform: Health, Feminism, and Bloomers

Not all women of the 1850s wore dresses with enormous hooped skirts. In the late 1840s, health journals, like the *Water Cure Journal*, began to encourage women to adopt a form of dress that was more conducive to good health. Rather than the constrictive corsets and heavy petticoats that were presently in fashion, some women of the early 1850s donned reform dress. Also called Freedom dress, Oriental dress, or Turkish dress, the ensemble consisted of a bodice and short, knee-length skirt over Turkish trousers.

In early 1851, this radical – though certainly more functional – way of dressing was adopted by American dress reformers and women's rights advocates, including Elizabeth Smith Miller, Elizabeth Cady Stanton, and Amelia Jenks Bloomer. Bloomer not only wore Turkish dress, she began to promote it in her magazine, the *Lily*. The *Lily* was the first magazine to be edited by a woman and focused primarily on issues relating to temperance, suffrage, women's rights, and dress reform.[3] It was not too much longer before Turkish dress began to be popularly known as Bloomer dress, Bloomer costume, or—quite simply—as Bloomers.

That same year, dress reformers in the United Kingdom began touting the many benefits of Bloomers. In September of 1851, Mrs C.H. Dexter delivered a lecture on 'Bloomerism' to a packed hall of men and women in Fitzroy Square, London. According to the 16 September 1851 edition of the *Morning Chronicle*:

> *'Her attire, which was wholly composed of black satin, consisted of a jacket ordinarily worn by ladies in walking dress, a skirt below that, scarcely reaching down to the knee, and a pair of exceedingly wide trousers, tied at the ankle.'*

Reform dress was often ridiculed, both by the public and in the Victorian press. (The Bloomer Costume, lithograph, Currier and Ives, 1851. Library of Congress)

THE BLOOMER COSTUME.

Mrs Dexter asserted that, as long as women's dress 'offered no violence to health or modesty,' she should 'be left at perfect liberty to consult her own taste in the matter of decoration, and her own feelings with regard to convenience and comfort'. Though this sentiment may have met with applause in the moment, in the larger sphere of Victorian life, Bloomers were seen as being slightly subversive. They were derided and ridiculed in the press and were often made the subject of comic songs and cartoons.

As for British fashion publications of the 1850s, they could not admit to Bloomers being anything more than an American oddity. An 1851 edition of the *London and Paris Ladies' Magazine of Fashion* states that 'we doubt very much that our American belles will find many imitators in the Old World,' reminding their readers that 'Paris lends fashion all over the world, and to her alone do we look for changes'.

Victorian Invention: Sewing Machines, Paper Patterns, and Aniline Dyes

In addition to the invention of the wire cage crinoline, the 1850s was notable for three other important, fashion-related innovations. The first was the sewing machine. Widely considered to be a Victorian era invention, the sewing machine was, in fact, a distant descendant of a mid-eighteenth century embroidery machine invented by Charles Frederick Weisenthal. Sewing machines would continue to appear in some form or another well into the early nineteenth century, but it was not until the Victorian era that the sewing machine as we know it today began to emerge on the scene.

Originally patented by American inventors Elias Howe in 1846 and Isaac Singer in 1851, the modern sewing machine was, first and foremost, an industrial tool. It was used primarily in factories, tailors' shops, and dressmaking establishments. But though it accelerated the speed of their work, the arrival of the sewing machine did little to improve the lot of poor working seamstresses. Instead, it led to mass production of clothing in factories where the working conditions were often quite grim – and sometimes even fatal.

In 1856, Singer introduced the first sewing machine for domestic use. It was an extraordinarily useful tool for ladies, many of whom used it not only for household sewing, but also for making their own clothing. Able to stitch one yard per minute in its earliest incarnation, it greatly sped up the process of sewing straight seams and was – as author Ella Rodman Church states in her 1882 book *The Home Needle* – a 'valuable aid in lightening the sewing of a household'.

The second fashion-related innovation of the 1850s was the paper dress pattern. The first paper pattern offered to the public came in the August 1850 edition of the *World of Fashion*. Soon other lady's magazines, in both Britain and the United States, began to follow suit, offering their readers patterns for dresses, skirts, bodices, and sleeves. When coupled with the invention of the sewing machine, the paper pattern allowed women to make the latest styles for themselves at a much lower price than that charged by a fashionable dressmaker or modiste.

Another significant fashion innovation of the decade was the discovery and subsequent utilization of aniline dyes. The first aniline dye, known as mauveine or aniline violet, was discovered by William Henry Perkin in 1856. Made from a distillation of coal-tar, it produced a brilliant purple colour which could be used to dye fabric. Perkin patented mauveine in 1858. More colours followed and, soon, women of every class were able to purchase gowns in bright reds, blues, yellows, and purples. Unlike the soft, faded colours produced by natural dyes—which were derived from plants, animals, and minerals—aniline dyes produced colours that were rich, vibrant, and of infinite variation.

Victorian Department Stores: Fixed Prices, Entrée Libre, and Ready-to-Wear

In 1852, French entrepreneur Aristide Boucicaut opened the first department store in Paris. Called *Le Bon Marché*, it offered customers a more welcoming shopping experience, with sales clerks who were helpful and friendly, even to those who were not wealthy or aristocratic. *Le Bon Marché* was one of the first retail establishments to offer fixed prices and a policy of *entrée libre*, or 'no obligation to buy'. It was also one of the first to offer seasonal sales and to allow customers to return items which they found unsatisfactory.

Other department stores soon opened in both London and New York. Like *Le Bon Marché*, they offered reasonably priced fabrics, as well as fashion accessories like gloves, fans, and millinery. They also offered some ready-to-wear clothing, including ladies' corsets, petticoats, and crinolines. By the end of the century, clothing sizes had become standardized and inventions like the sewing machine and the cutting machine – which could cut eighteen layers of fabric at a time – greatly sped up the process of making ladies' clothing. This enabled department stores to offer an even greater selection of ready-to-wear garments such as skirts, shirts, and dresses for both day and evening.

Department stores had a democratizing effect on fashion, making stylish clothing and accessories available to a wider class of women. Unfortunately, though many other pieces of clothing could be made ready-to-wear, the most fashionable dresses of the period still required hours of hand sewing, making them quite costly to purchase and keeping them far out of reach for any but the wealthiest members of society.

Chapter 3

The 1860s

'The ball-dresses are noticeable for an excess of ornamental work, and designs of much intricacy, involving great labour; however, as the sewing-machine has now arrived at such a perfect state of utility, this is not surprising.'

The London and Paris Ladies' Magazine of Fashion, 1866.

The 1860s was one of the most significant decades in nineteenth century women's fashion. It began with skirts having reached their maximum size of the century and ended with the yards of fabric that had once been draped over enormous wire crinolines being drawn to the back and draped over a wire bustle. This was a dramatic change in silhouette, further accentuated by the popularity of tightly laced corsets, trained skirts, and the gradual raising of hemlines to expose a lady's feet—and her ankles!

This was also the decade of the American Civil War, a conflict which took place over the course of four years and claimed the lives of more than 620,000 people. The war had a significant effect on the fashionable dress of American women, particularly those women residing in the war-torn South.

The 1860s Silhouette

Beginning the decade, the majority of women's gowns were now machine made and – thanks to the discovery of aniline dyes – fabrics came in a new range of vivid colours, including mauve and magenta. Meanwhile, crinolines were at their absolute largest, with hemlines reaching as much as ten to fifteen feet in circumference. But though large skirts were still all the rage, the first signs of change were gradually becoming visible. Women's skirts were now slightly gored on each side, a practice which lessened the width of the skirt at the top while keeping the width at the bottom. This had the effect of flattening the front and throwing the fullness of the skirts to the back.

As women became more active, additional gores were added to their skirts to accommodate their movement. When coupled with the fashion for dresses that were worn longer in the back, an 1861 edition of *Godey's Lady's Book* explains that this goring caused the lower part of a lady's skirts to 'spread well and form a train'. By 1863, the *Englishwoman's Domestic Magazine* was reporting that fashionable dresses were now generally made with 'perfect trains behind'. It was an elegant style in the drawing room, but for walking about the dirty streets of town, trains were far from practical. To prevent them from becoming soiled, the *Englishwoman's Domestic Magazine* advises that:

> *'If ladies will be in the fashion, and wear trained skirts in the streets, in dirty weather, they may keep them in order by wearing them looped up over a pretty petticoat.'*

The fashion for looping up trained skirts and securing them with cords, tassels, or ribbons resulted in women wearing richer and more elaborate petticoats. The *Englishwoman's Domestic Magazine* even went so far as to predict that it would 'soon be necessary to have the petticoat made as handsome as the dress'.

For daywear, the early 1860s saw the emergence of skirts paired with blouses. The Garibaldi shirt was particularly popular. Named for the loose-fitting, scarlet shirts worn by the men who followed Italian revolutionary Giuseppe Garibaldi, the Garibaldi shirt was originally made of red merino wool trimmed in black braid, cord, and buttons. The 1861 edition of the *Englishwoman's Domestic Magazine* describes a typical Garibaldi shirt, as featured in one of their December fashion plates:

> *'The Garibaldi shirt – an article that is now so much in favour – is made of very bright scarlet French merino, braided with black, and fastened down the front by black merino buttons. The shirt is made with a narrow collar, and straps on the shoulders, ornamented with braid, and a narrow black silk cravat is worn underneath the collar. The sleeves are gathered into a wristband, also braided, fastened by means of buttons and loops.'*

Garibaldi shirts were available in other colours and fabrics as well. They could be made of cotton, linen, silk or – as an 1862 edition of *Godey's Lady's Book* reports – 'printed flannel, merino, muslin de laine, printed cambric, foulard, or pique'. White muslin Garibaldi shirts were especially fashionable and could often be seen paired with colourful silk skirts.

A variant of the Garibaldi shirt was the short, open-front Garibaldi jacket which fastened at the neck. It was similarly made in scarlet wool with military trimming, but could also be seen in a wide range of fabrics and in colours as varied as brown, blue, purple, and even pink.

Garibaldi shirts and jackets were not the only pieces of early 1860s women's clothing with a military pedigree. Lightweight, collarless Zouave jackets and vests, which were inspired by the uniforms worn by Algerian soldiers in the Italian war of 1859, were also considered quite fashionable. The Zouave was waist-length or

A fashion plate showing a red Garibaldi shirt (left) and a ball gown worn with a colored petticoat. (*Englishwoman's Domestic Magazine*, 1861)

shorter with an open, rounded front that curved toward the back. It fastened at the neck and, in its jacket form, had wide, long sleeves.

Zouaves of the 1860s were made of silk, velvet, cashmere, or cloth and trimmed in dark-coloured braid. For day dress, they were generally made to match a lady's skirts and could be worn over either a Garibaldi blouse, a long-sleeved muslin chemisette, or an embroidered waistcoat. The combination of short jacket and waistcoat would continue to be popular for several years and, by 1863, the *Englishwoman's Domestic Magazine* was declaring that 'fancy jackets and waistcoats appear to be more in vogue than ever.'

In day dresses, sleeves of the early 1860s saw very little change from those of the late 1850s. Pagoda or bell-shaped sleeves with false undersleeves were still widely worn, as were close fitting long sleeves that ended at the wrist. Bodices remained tight to the shape. They were high at the neck and typically fastened in the front with a row of buttons – a practical feature which made it much easier for a lady to dress herself without assistance.

A lady (right) wearing a Zouave jacket with a waistcoat and matching skirt. (*Les Modes Parisiennes*, 1863. Thomas J. Watson Library, Metropolitan Museum of Art)

Day dresses were often accessorized with a detachable collar and cuffs. Made of white linen or cotton, they could be removed when soiled and washed right along with a lady's false undersleeves, chemise, and drawers. Swiss belts were another popular accessory for 1860s day dresses. Generally black in colour, they curved to a point both above and below the centre front and back of the waist.

For evening dress, gowns were cut low off the shoulder. Necklines were *en coeur* and were often draped with a bertha collar for modesty. Ball gowns of the early 1860s were far more daring, with necklines cut low both in the front and, occasionally, in the back. Sleeves were short, with bare arms adding to the overall picture of bare shoulders and the glimpse of bosom which was often revealed by a fashionable ball gown's square or V-shaped décolletage. Most fashionable ball gowns of this period had double skirts and were elaborately trimmed with lace, ostrich plumes, swansdown, or garlands of flowers.

When it came to fabrics of the early 1860s, ladies were rather spoiled for choice. For daywear, there were terry velvets and poplins. While for eveningwear, the 1861 edition of *Godey's Lady's Book* states:

> '*For young ladies, thulle [sic], white and colored crape, gauze, tarleton, and other diaphanous fabrics, are the most suitable. Still, the rich silks in stripes of contrasting high colors, in moire, and particularly watered silks, in stripes of large and small waves, or brocaded silks with plain grounds, and Jacquarded figures, seem to be most sought after.*'

By the mid-1860s, the fashion for looping up the skirts to reveal the decorative petticoat underneath had generally fallen by the wayside. However, some examples of it can still be seen in both British and American ladies' magazines of that period. For example, one image from the 1866 edition of the *Englishwoman's Domestic Magazine*, shows a morning promenade dress with grey poplin skirts that have been 'looped up with tirettes composed of velvet and steel, and fastened with steel buckles' to reveal the crimson petticoat beneath. Tirettes were cords which were sewn underneath the bottom of a lady's skirts. The cords could then be drawn up at the waist to raise the skirts above the petticoat.

Gored skirts with trains continued to dominate women's fashionable dress well into the mid- to late 1860s, leading the 1866 edition of the *Englishwoman's Domestic Magazine* to report:

> '*The one universal law imposed by fashion at present is that of the gored skirt. It gives great elegance to the figure, throwing all the fullness of the dress to the back, so as to form a graceful train, while in front the dress is quite plain, and short enough to let the feet show.*'

Drawing further attention to the back of a woman's figure was the addition of a peplum or short, overskirt attached to the waist of a dress or jacket. Peplums were worn for both day and evening and were often ornately trimmed. The 1866 and 1867 editions of the *London and Paris Ladies' Magazine of Fashion* describe several styles that were fashionable, including peplums trimmed with ribbon, crystal beads, or pearls, and peplums edged with tassels, fringe, or Valenciennes lace.

An excess of trimming was a feature of many mid- to late-1860s dresses, especially those for evening. Describing the ball dresses of 1866, the *London and Paris Ladies' Magazine,* writes:

A fashion plate showing a skirt looped up with tirettes to reveal a coloured petticoat. (*Englishwoman's Domestic Magazine*, 1866)

'The ball-dresses are noticeable for an excess of ornamental work, and designs of much intricacy, involving great labour; however, as the sewing-machine has now arrived at such a perfect state of utility, this is not surprising.'

As the decade progressed, two distinct classes of day dress began to emerge: walking or promenade dresses and afternoon or visiting dresses. Walking dresses were made high at the throat. They had shorter skirts and did not have a train, making them ideal for a stroll in the park or a walk into town. By contrast, afternoon dresses were made of richer fabrics, with square necklines and long, sweeping trains that generally fell eighty inches from waist to floor. They were suitable for carriage drives and formal visits – basically anywhere that did not require a great deal of walking!

By the close of the decade, the focus of women's dress was almost entirely at the back. Trains began to be embellished with pleats, ribbons, bows, silk fringe, tassels, and decorative buttons and overskirts were gathered and drawn back into what was known as a pannier puff, a style reminiscent of fashions worn at the

A day dress (left) and a ball gown with a ruffled train. (*Journal des Demoiselles*, 1869. Thomas J. Watson Library, Metropolitan Museum of Art)

court of Louis XV of France. At the same time, the fad for tight lacing re-emerged. Women cinched themselves into heavily adorned bodices, their narrow waists often accentuated with a close-fitting belt or a ribbon sash which terminated in a large bow at the back.

For day dresses, sleeves were narrow and close to the arm, while for ball gowns sleeves all but disappeared. Instead, ball gowns were often attached at the shoulder with delicate straps or ribbon bows. They had low necklines and double or triple skirts which were looped up and trimmed with flounces of lace, ribbons, or garlands of flowers. *Godey's Lady's Book* describes a particularly fashionable, flower-trimmed ball gown worn by the Princess of Wales in 1869, writing:

> 'The Princess of Wales wore a white tulle dress; the skirt was bouillonné [shirred], and ornamented with three exquisite garlands of roses and their buds; these were arranged as a fringe upon the skirt, and described wide festoons. There was a fringe of roses upon the bodice, and the sash was pink gros grain.'

THE 1860s

Undergarments: Crinolettes and Steam-Moulded Corsets

With gored skirts continually moving the fullness of a lady's dress toward the back, it was necessary that crinolines be altered to fit. An article in the 1860 edition of *Godey's Lady's Book* reports that 'the best people' preferred 'the trailing bell shape' of a wire crinoline. Crinolines would continue to change in both shape and size and, by the end of the decade, had transformed into the crinolette. The crinolette was small and consisted of half hoops and horsehair flounces only at the back which served to support a lady's draped skirts and train.

As the size of women's skirts shrank, corsets became tighter and less forgiving. In 1868, Edwin Izod invented the process of steam-moulding. Corsets were sprayed wet with starch, stretched tight over steam-heated iron torso moulds, and dried into shape. This resulted in corsets that were more curvaceous. They were also stiffer, more restrictive, and strong enough to squeeze women's bodies into the desired hourglass silhouette without breaking.

Millinery: Spoon Bonnets, Pork Pies, and Empress Hats

Fashionable bonnets of the 1860s were smaller than in the previous decade, with brims tilted upward on the forehead and wide, silk ribbons that tied under the chin in large, stylish bows. In the early 1860s, the most popular bonnet of this variety was the spoon bonnet, which curved high above the forehead in a spoon-shaped peak. Spoon bonnets fell in for their fair share of ridicule. In 1865, when the style began to fall from favour, *Punch* even published an 'Ode on the Burial of the Spoon-Bonnet,' which reads in part:

> *'Lay the Spoon-bonnet low!*
> *And be its silk watered with tearful brine*
> *And bid it happy-speed*
> *To the Elysian mead*
> *Where the departed Fashions shine.'*

Bonnets would continue to shrink in size and, by 1866, the *Englishwoman's Domestic Magazine* was reporting that 'the crown, curtain, and cap' had all disappeared, leaving nothing of the bonnet but 'a narrow fanchon border, rounded in front and coming just a little over the forehead.' This fashionable, but miniscule chapeau was called the fanchon bonnet, a style that was generally made of straw, tulle, silk, or velvet and ornamented with ribbons, lace, silk flowers, foliage, feathers, or beads.

By 1865, hats were gradually beginning to surpass bonnets in popularity. One of the most popular was the pork pie hat. Pork pies were small and round with flat crowns and narrow, turned up brims. The Empress hat was also considered quite fashionable. Named after the Empress Eugénie, it had a flat crown with a turned-up brim and was worn tilted forward at a jaunty angle over the forehead. Pork pies and Empress hats came in a range of materials, including straw, silk, felt, and velvet.

Some fashionable styles of hat worn in the 1860s were a revival of styles worn in the eighteenth century. One of these was the straw *bergère* or shepherdess hat. Bergère hats were usually made of straw and had low, shallow crowns and wide, flat brims. They could be ornamented with ribbons or flowers.

Footwear: Velvet Boots, Dyed Satin Pumps, and Louis XV Heels.

Women's dresses and hats were not the only articles of clothing in the 1860s to take inspiration from eighteenth century France. Elements of eighteenth century style extended to women's evening shoes as well. The 1869 edition of the *New Monthly Belle Assemblée* describes a pair of 'Dauphine shoes' made of 'green gros-grain silk with a square bow of black lace' and a pair of evening pumps with 'Louis XV heels made of white satin with a blond rosette.' Evening pumps were generally made of silk or satin with low heels and slightly squared toes. They were often dyed to match a lady's evening dress and featured embellishments such as rosettes, bows, beads, embroidery, and lace.

For daywear, most ladies wore ankle-length boots which fastened with laces or buttons. In the early 1860s, elastic gored Congress boots and other practical styles were still being sold. Most were lined with cloth or flannel and had soles and heels that were half an inch thick. However, as looped skirts began to reveal women's feet to all and sundry, boots could no longer be merely serviceable. They had to be dainty and attractive as well. Describing a few of the latest styles in Paris, the 1864 edition of *Godey's Lady's Book* reports:

> *'For damp, rainy weather small buttoned kid boots, with tassels are worn; also French satin boots, likewise buttoned, and trimmed with Astrakan fur up the front and round the ankle.'*

When the weather was fine, fashionable ladies preferred 'black velvet boots, embroidered with white silk' or boots of French satin with mother-of-pearl buttons. Boots of red morocco leather were also worn, as were boots of Russia leather and gilt or bronze kid.

Outerwear: The Paletot and the Pardessus

Cloaks and mantles continued to be worn as outerwear throughout the 1860s. Loose-fitting coats of varying lengths were also quite popular. When made short, these coats were called *paletots*. They were very slightly fitted at the waist and had long, wide sleeves. The 1863 edition of *Le Follett* describes several styles of *paletot* which were fashionable that year, including the hooded *Paletot Frivoline* which was made of velvet trimmed with swansdown. For daywear, *Le Follet* reports that morning toilettes were 'generally made *en suite*' with the dress, paletot, and petticoat all cut from the same material and trimmed to correspond.

Another variety of coat was the *pardessus*. First introduced in the 1840s, the *pardessus* was generally longer and closer fitting than the *paletot*, with wide, roomy sleeves and an open front which fastened closed from the waist to the throat. It could be made of cloth, corded silk, or velvet and was often trimmed with velvet, fur, or lace. Like the paletot, the *pardessus* came in many different styles with a bewildering array of names – most of which depended on the ladies' magazine in which they were featured. For example, the 1862 edition of the *Englishwomen's Domestic Magazine* describes a style of *pardessus* called the *Pardessus Monténégrin* which was made of 'black velvet, ornamented at the edge with bands of sable'. There was also the *Hungarian Pardessus* made of 'black silk, trimmed with gimp rosettes on the body and sleeves' and the *Polish Pardessus* which fitted tight at the back and loose at the front.

Accessories: Cashmere Gloves, Pocket-Handkerchiefs, and French Sable Muffs

The most fashionable gloves of the 1860s were made of light-coloured kid with one or two small buttons at the wrist and delicate embroidery at the back of the hand. For everyday wear, cashmere gloves were the most suitable. The 1861 edition of the *Englishwomen's Domestic Magazine* describes several styles of note, including cashmere gloves that were 'embroidered at the back, and finished by a little silk acorn' and cashmere gloves with a gauntlet cuff made in two shades of plush which 'fastened underneath by a button.' There were also grey cashmere gloves embroidered with violet that were accented with 'rows of violet and lilac plush, and fastened with a violet button'.

Most fashionable ladies of the 1860s carried a pocket-handkerchief made of fine muslin or lace. According to the 1861 edition of *Godey's Lady's Book*, the most elaborate of these were 'a mere mass of cobwebby lace, of no use to anybody in particular, not even to the owner'. For ordinary use, a plain handkerchief neatly trimmed with lace or elegantly embroidered with a lady's initials in the corner was quite sufficient. If a lady could not afford a real lace trimming, she was on no account to use a cotton lace substitute. The 1860 edition of *Godey's Lady's Book* calls handkerchiefs trimmed in cotton lace 'the extreme of vulgar pretension'. Instead, ladies lacking the funds for real lace were advised to hem their handkerchiefs with a simple scalloped border.

In colder weather, many ladies employed a muff to keep their hands warm. Muffs of the 1860s were worn suspended from the neck by a tasselled cord. The most fashionable were generally made of French or Russian sable, richly trimmed mink, or ermine edged with swan's-down. By the mid-1860s, smaller muffs were becoming quite popular, as were muffs in odd shapes with pockets and fur flaps. The 1865 edition of the *Ladies' Companion and Monthly Magazine* describes one such muff which appeared on the Parisian fashion scene that season:

> *'The back is flat, and formed of velvet, or leather, and contains a pocket for money – a convenience you will allow, and also a security. The front, which is of fur, has a lap formed of the head of the animal which, on being raised, discloses another pocket, lined with satin, and intended for the pocket-handkerchief. This elaborate affair is suspended from the neck by a rich cord, with tassels, which falls over the front. Our Correspondent describes this new muff as the prettiest and most ravissante affair possible.'*

Jewellery: Matching Sets, Mourning Lockets, and Hair Brooches

Fashionable ladies of the 1860s wore earrings, rings, bracelets, brooches, and necklaces made in a diverse range of styles and materials. For daywear, the 1864 edition of the *Englishwomen's Domestic Magazine* advises its readers that jewellery should be kept 'very quiet in appearance,' stating that 'a set of the same is in better taste than a mixture of different kinds'. To that end, matching sets of hair combs, earrings, and necklaces – often made in rock crystal or steel – were considered to be essential to a morning toilette. A matching bracelet, chatelaine, and buttons could also be added.

For evening and full dress, ladies donned jewellery set with emeralds, amethysts, aquamarines, agates, or lapis lazuli. According to the *Englishwomen's Domestic Magazine*, the most fashionable earrings were 'formed of one large ball supporting three others attached by chains'. These dainty, ball earrings were often complimented by a necklace which was wound 'at least twice round the neck'.

The death of Prince Albert in 1861 coupled with the outbreak of the American Civil War spurred on a fashion for mourning jewellery in both Britain and America. Ladies in mourning often wore brooches, bracelets, and rings which were made – at least in part – of human hair. Some chose to wear a cameo or a black mourning locket containing an image of their deceased loved one or a lock of their loved one's hair. Others favoured brooches and earrings made of onyx or jet. For the latter stages of mourning, ladies were permitted to wear jewellery made of amethyst.

THE 1860s

Empress Eugénie, Charles Worth, and the Birth of Haute Couture

Empress Eugénie was the ultimate arbiter of fashion in mid-nineteenth century France. In the early 1850s, it was her preference for enormous skirts which set off the crinoline era. And, in the early 1860s, when Eugénie began to wear gowns made by Paris designer Charles Frederick Worth, the fashionable world sat up and took notice.

An Englishman born and bred, Worth moved to France in 1845. In 1858, after a successful stint as a cutter at Gagelin's accessories shop in Paris, he opened his own salon in the Rue de la Paix in partnership with Swedish businessman Otto Gustave. He soon earned a reputation as the most fashionable – and most exclusive – dress designer in Europe. Wealthy women of fashion flocked to his salon, all desiring one of Worth's elegant, hand-sewn creations of their own. One of these women, the Princesse Pauline de Metternich Sandor, was instrumental in bringing Worth to the attention of the Empress Eugénie and it was not long before the Empress extended her patronage.

Worth revolutionized dressmaking. In addition to using lavish fabrics and trimmings to create an idealized female figure, he was the first to use live models to showcase his work, the first to offer new collections each year, and the first to sign his work with a label. Today he is known as the Father of Haute Couture. In the nineteenth century, however, he was known simply for the stunning beauty of his creations. As one Victorian newspaper article so aptly explains:

'If ladies think of him, it is but as the embodiment of a power from which comes conquests in the ball-room and glory at every fashionable gathering; to prosaic men his is a hated name suggestive of long bills and financial ruin.'[5]

The Dark Side of Dressmaking: The Tragedy of Mary Walkley

At the same time that Charles Frederick Worth was gaining fame as couturier to the Empress Eugénie, a darker side of dressmaking was being exposed to the Victorian public. On 17 June 1863, *The Times* printed a letter which shone a harsh light on the miserable work and living conditions of seamstresses, not in the East End of London, but in one of the finest dressmaking establishments in London's West End.

The letter was written by a young woman who signed herself simply as 'A Tired Dressmaker.' She began by writing:

'Sir, - I am a dressmaker, living in a large West-end house of business. I work in a crowded room with twenty-eight others. This morning one of my companions was found dead in her bed, and we all of us think that long hours and close confinement have had a great deal to do with her end.'

The letter went on to describe the circumstances leading to the death of twenty-year-old seamstress Mary Walkley. Walkley was in the employ of a court dressmaker who went by the name of Madame Elise. Located at 170 Regent Street, Madame Elise's shop catered to the most fashionable ladies in London society. In order to meet their exacting demands, the seamstresses who lived and worked on the premises were obliged to begin their day at half-past six in the morning and work straight through until eleven at night. On some occasions – such as those days preceding a Queen's drawing-room or other major society event – they were even required to work all night and into the next morning to finish an order.

When the seamstresses were finally permitted to retire to bed, they found little respite. Describing the suffocating accommodations at Madame Elise's establishment, the 'Tired Dressmaker' writes:

> *'At night we retire to rest in a room divided into little cells, each just large enough to contain two beds. There are two of us in each bed. There is no ventilation; I could scarcely breathe in them when I first came from the country. The doctor who came this morning said they were not fit for dogs to sleep in.'*

Mary Walkley took ill on a Friday. By Sunday she was worse. The other seamstresses at Madame Elise's sat up with her that night until she fell asleep. The next morning, Mary Walkley's bedfellow woke to find Mary dead beside her.

The death of Mary Walkley sparked a firestorm of public outrage. People were horrified by the conditions under which West End seamstresses lived and worked. Many argued for reforms, including strict regulations governing the workrooms. Others wanted Madame Elise and her husband to be prosecuted for their perceived role in Mary's death. The scandal even prompted the 4 July 1863 edition of *Punch* to publish a cartoon titled 'The Haunted Lady, or The Ghost in the Looking Glass' which shows a fashionable young woman admiring her new gown in the mirror only to see the reflection of the seamstress who died in the process of making it.

The fact that many of the young seamstresses employed at establishments like that of Madame Elise were orphans or girls who had fallen on hard times made their working conditions that much more despicable in the public view. Some even compared the exploitation of vulnerable seamstresses to a form of slavery. As an article in the 27 June 1863 edition of the *Preston Chronicle* states:

> *'We should even now have been unaware of the extent to which "white slavery" exists at the west end of London had not this poor girl died under circumstances which caused an investigation by a coroner.'*

The inquest into the death of Mary Walkley received a great deal of public attention. Ultimately, the jury found that Mary had died of apoplexy, likely accelerated by overwork and poor ventilation. Those who had hoped for Madame Elise and her

THE HAUNTED LADY, OR "THE GHOST" IN THE LOOKING-GLASS.

Madame La Modiste. "WE WOULD NOT HAVE DISAPPOINTED YOUR LADYSHIP, AT ANY SACRIFICE, AND THE ROBE IS FINISHED *À MERVEILLE*"

A grim cartoon inspired by the death of Mary Walkley. ('Ghost in the Looking Glass' by John Tenniel for *Punch*, 1863)

husband to be charged with murder were deeply disappointed. An article in the 2 July 1863 edition of the *Stirling Observer* calls the verdict dissatisfying in the extreme, declaring:

> *'If to work seventeen and eighteen hours a-day all the year round; to be allowed no out-door exercise or spare time at dinner or tea, but just sufficient to take hurried meals, and then, after slaving at the needle till eye and hand fails, and head and heart grow sick, to be marched off to "dens" four abreast, where throughout the short night, instead of being refreshed by "tired Nature's sweet restorer – balmy sleep," they are stifled with the venom of carbonic acid gas, and other active impure agents in bad ventilation – If master or mistress in any millinery or other establishment in the kingdom, compels his or her employees to undergo such an ordeal, or else go without work, in the sight of God and man, nay, according to a fair and just interpretation of the law of the land, they are as deliberately taking away life by slow poison, as sure and deadly in its work as that by which L'Angelier met his death. If that is not murder, what is it?'*

In response to Mary Walkley's death, the Earl of Shaftesbury brought the matter before the House of Lords. He asked if the Government would 'bring a bill to provide for the sanitary regulations of the workrooms in which seamstresses were employed,' pointing out that the Legislature had 'already granted similar relief in other occupations'.[6] However, despite the public outcry over the working conditions of West End seamstresses, no Victorian era laws were enacted to regulate their hours and working conditions. Even if they had been, they would have been difficult to enforce as dressmakers worked in private establishments which were not open to government inspectors.

Fashion and the American Civil War

The American Civil War took place from 1861-5. During that time, the Southern states were essentially cut off from those in the North. They were equally cut off from the newest fashions. Southern ports were blockaded and it was almost impossible for supplies from the North – including the latest in fashionable apparel and accessories – to get through. As a result, Southern women generally made do with what they had. They remade old gowns, repurposed textiles, and mixed and matched bodices and jackets with skirts. Some women even attempted to weave their own fabric.

Northern women still had access to the latest styles from London and Paris, but interest in fashionable clothing was not what it had been before the war. With the men away fighting, both Northern and Southern women shouldered additional responsibilities at home and in their communities. They formed ladies' aid societies, volunteered as nurses, and cooked and sewed for the troops. Many women were in mourning for husbands, brothers, and fathers. They remained in seclusion, garbed in black gowns trimmed in jet and wearing veils to hide their faces.

Frugality and simplicity were the order of the day. Rather than heavily trimmed day dresses and evening dresses, American ladies' magazines of the period, such as *Peterson's Magazine* and *Godey's Lady's Book*, encouraged women to wear plain garments that were easily adaptable. Extravagance in dress was frowned upon during the war, with some viewing fashionable excess as being unpatriotic. As an 1864 issue of *Arthur's Home Magazine* proclaims:

'When we see a lady on the street extravagantly dressed, and displaying her costly adornment, we are forced to think she is one of the number who love self more than country.'

Chapter 4

The 1870s

'The present fashions for ladies are far more graceful and becoming than they have been since the commencement of the century.'
The Milliner and Dressmaker and Warehouseman's Gazette, 1870.

The 1870s ushered in an era of sleek, sensuous gowns that accented every curve. Gone were the enormous crinolines of the 1860s. In their place were figure-hugging frocks with low-set trains that fanned out like a peacock's tail. This was the decade of tight lacing, tea gowns, and tassel-trimmed skirts in shimmering silk brocades. This was also the decade that marked an end to the Second Empire and ushered in *La Belle Époque* in Europe, a period of prosperity, optimism, and innovation.

The 1870s Silhouette

Beginning the decade, the general size of ladies' gowns was slimmer and simpler than in the previous years. Trimmings, however, had grown more elaborate and, with the addition of tassels, fringe, buttons, bows, velvet, and braid, fashionable gowns began to bear more than a passing resemblance to lavish draperies or richly upholstered furnishings.

In 1870, the Franco-Prussian War put an end to the Second Empire. It also put an end to Empress Eugénie's reign as the leader of the fashionable world. When France was defeated in 1871, Eugénie fled to England where she proceeded to live a comparatively quiet life. No longer able to look to the French Empress and her court for guidance, the fashionable world began to take inspiration from history, drawing on elements of sixteenth, seventeenth, and eighteenth century style.

In day dresses, necklines were high, bodices remained close to the shape, and tight sleeves were gradually giving way to wide Pagoda sleeves. The 1870 edition of the *Milliner and Dressmaker and Warehouseman's Gazette* reports that fashionable day dresses of serge, poplin, and cashmere were frequently made with jacket bodices, some of which were trimmed 'to simulate an open jacket over a waistcoat.'

Day dresses were generally made with two skirts – an underskirt and an overskirt. According to the *Milliner and Dressmaker*, the underskirt was made with 'one or more flounces,' while the overskirt was worn 'either open in front as a tunic, or made like a sort of apron, plain in front and rounded off at the sides.' Overskirts of the early 1870s were drawn up and back, but instead of being formed into a puff, they were now draped over a soft bustle made of straw or meshed horsehair from which they cascaded down to form an elegant train.

For evening, dresses of the early 1870s followed the same basic shape as day dresses, fitting slim on the body, with the fullness of the skirts drawn to the back. They came in a variety of styles. There were silk and satin dinner and theatre dresses, opera dresses with low, square necklines, and ball gowns made of tulle and lace. Many evening dresses with low necklines were made with collarettes. The Medici collarette, which consisted of 'deep lace standing-up behind, and spreading like a fan' was particularly popular.[7]

Most evening dresses had either short, puffed sleeves or elbow-length sleeves trimmed with a deep frill or flounce of lace. Ball gowns were cut low off the shoulder both in the front and in the back and had either a rounded, square, or a V-shaped neckline. Underskirts of ball gowns were often made in stripes of contrasting colour or fabric and edged in pleats or a flounce. Overskirts were drawn back over a soft bustle and, along with the train, could be ornamented in a variety of trimmings, including lace, fringe, ribbons, or bows.

In 1871, there was a revival of the eighteenth century French polonaise. Cunnington describes the style as consisting of 'a bodice and tunic in one, the tunic being looped up at the sides, short in front and much looped up behind into a puff'.

Fashionable ball gowns of the early 1870s. (*Le Monde Elegant*, December 1870. Thomas J. Watson Library, Metropolitan Museum of Art)

When made with floral printed silk, it was popularly known as the 'Dolly Varden,' after a character in Charles Dickens' novel *Barnaby Rudge*. The polonaise could be worn for both day and evening and provided a fashionable alternative to the two-piece combination of overskirt and bodice.

As the decade progressed, trimmings became even more excessive. Skirts were flounced, puffed, and pleated, with the flounces, puffs, and pleats often embellished with piping and trimmings of their own. Ball gowns were frequently trimmed with flowers. The 1873 edition of the *London and Paris Ladies' Magazine of Fashion* describes one fashionable ball gown of the season made with an underskirt of white muslin and blue silk and an overskirt of blue silk which is caught up and fastened with bouquets of roses, writing:

> *'The caught-up portions of upper skirt are fastened at the juncture of these points, by bouquets of roses having trails, and united by a garland. The opening in front of the skirt is crossed by three garlands of leaves with buds. The corsage [bodice] is trimmed a bretelles, by similar garlands terminated at the back and front of waist by single roses, and on each shoulder is a rose, the space between the garlands being filled in both at back and in front, by four quillings of white muslin.'*

In 1874, the cuirasse bodice was introduced. Named for a close-fitting piece of defensive armour which covered a soldier's torso, the cuirasse bodice extended down tight over a lady's hips. At the same time, dresses were being made more closely around the front and overskirts began to be tied back, a practice which created a slinky mermaid's tail train. This new form-fitting style was not without its detractors. Many Victorians objected to what they considered an indecent, overly sensualized style of dress, with some comparing the new fashions in gowns to a woman appearing in public in nothing but her undergarments.

As in the crinoline era, public criticism did little to stem the tide of fashion. Ladies' dresses continued to be worn tight to the shape, with long cuirasse bodices and basques stretching even further down over the hips. Soon, the fullness of the train could no longer start at the waist. Instead, the 1877 edition of the *London and Paris Ladies' Magazine of Fashion* reports that trains now commenced from just below the level of the long bodice or basque and then spread gradually out, taking 'a form which somewhat resembles a fan or a peacock's tail'.

This marked the beginning of what was known as the natural form era, a period which lasted from 1877-82. The natural form era was characterized by form-fitting cuirasse bodices with close-fitting sleeves and slim underskirts. Overskirts had become tighter as well and were often draped or folded at the back into intricate points and pleats. At this stage, the soft bustle disappeared, leaving behind only as much fullness at the back as could be created by the draped fabric of the skirts.

Also popular during the natural form era was the one-piece princess dress. Invented by Charles Worth, the princess dress did not have a waist seam. Instead,

During the natural form era, trains began just below the level of the long, tight-fitting bodice. (Natural Form Dresses, *Journal des Demoiselles*, 1877. Thomas J. Watson Library, Metropolitan Museum of Art)

it fell in one continuous piece of fabric from shoulder to hem and was fitted to the figure with vertical seams and darts.

In the middle of the decade, pockets became a feature of many fashionable day dresses. The 1876 issue of *Godey's Lady's Book* reports that some of these pockets were so large that they occupied the entire length of the skirt 'from belt to hem'. Bodices with lace-trimmed necklines were very much in favour in the mid-1870s, as were stand up collars. Skirts were ruffled, flounced, or pleated and, on some gowns, the overskirt draped tight across the hips and secured with decorative buttons or bows.

By 1878, overskirts had grown so long and tight that, on some dresses, false underskirts were being used. According to *Godey's Lady's Book*, these 'sham skirts' had once been objected to because they were apt to be exposed if the overskirt was blown up in a high wind. Now, however, overskirts were made to cling so closely to the legs that, as *Godey's* reports, 'the expense and weight of heavy woollen stuffs beneath it are dispensed with'.

As the decade came to a close, tea gowns began to come into fashion. Tea gowns were loosely fitted and could be worn without corsets. They were often donned by ladies for afternoons spent at home, either presiding over the tea tray or visiting with female friends. They first appeared on the fashion scene in 1877, but were initially criticized for being too much like ladies' dressing gowns. By 1879, they were becoming much more acceptable, especially when they were made to resemble the tight-fitting dresses that were so much in fashion.

Undergarments: Dress Improvers, Combinations, Spoon Busks, and Suspenders

The early 1870s silhouette was achieved, in part, by the use of a dress improver or soft bustle. Politely known as a *tournure*, the dress improver generally took the form of several layered rows of ruffled or pleated horsehair cloth. It tied on at the waist and was initially worn in combination with a crinolette.

In addition to horsehair cloth, dress improvers of the early 1870s were also available in a range of other – sometimes novel – materials. There were dress improvers made of padded cushions; others were made of fabric-covered wire, whalebone, sponge, and cork. One newspaper advertisement from 1874 even describes an 'airproof dress improver' which was made of 'light and durable' rubber that could be 'easily inflated' to whatever size best suited a lady's dress.[8]

By the end of 1875, fashion magazines and newspapers of the day were proclaiming the end of the dress improver. Slim, vertical lines were now *de rigeur* and dress improvers, it was said, had been 'banished from all well-appointed wardrobes'.[9] Fashionable Victorian ladies no longer desired to add volume at the back of their skirts. Instead, they were looking for ways to make their dresses fit even closer to the body. One such method was to replace their separate chemise and drawers with a less bulky one-piece undergarment called a combination. Combinations were relatively plain and could be made of knit, silk, or chamois leather. They allowed for a much smoother line underneath the formfitting dresses of the late 1870s.

Another essential component of the 1870s silhouette was the corset. As cuirasse bodices and princess dresses came into fashion, corsets grew longer, extending down to curve over the hips. In 1873, the spoon busk was introduced. Made of a shaped piece of steel that was narrow at the top and widened down to a pear-shaped bottom, it curved in at the waist to fit firmly over the abdomen. When combined with tight lacing, these longer, steam moulded corsets with spoon busks whittled women's waists to mere inches, creating an idealized hourglass shape that some began to fear was hazardous to a lady's health.

In 1878, elastic suspenders were introduced. Initially attached to a belt that was worn over the corset, they clipped to the tops of a lady's stockings, holding them up in place of garters. Suspenders were considered preferable to garters by many in the medical community who believed that tight garters impeded a lady's circulation. As an added benefit, suspenders also helped to hold long corsets in place.

Though many of the advances in women's undergarments were purely practical, women's underwear of the 1870s was becoming far less utilitarian in appearance. Undergarments began to be made in even finer fabrics, such as delicate cambrics, muslins, and silks. Chemises were now shaped to the bosom with seams, pleats, and darts. They were made in a variety of necklines to suit day and evening dresses and were often trimmed in embroidery or delicate bands of lace. Silk corsets were also frequently edged with lace and now came in a range of colours as diverse as red, blue, purple, yellow, and pink.

Millinery: Square-Crowned Hats, Coloured Straw Bonnets, and Follow-Me-Lads

Hats and bonnets of the 1870s came in a range of shapes and sizes. There was no one prevailing style of the decade; however, hats with square crowns and brims which were turned up either on one side or the other were very much in fashion, as were Tyrolean hats with high-pointed crowns and 'jaunty Derby hats precisely like those worn by gentlemen'.[10] Two popular styles from the early 1870s were the Medici and the Castilian. An 1873 edition of *Godey's Lady's Book* describes the Medici as having an 'ample brim projecting squarely over the forehead' with each side 'turned up high and close to the crown' and a back which descended into 'a very sharp point'. By contrast, the Castilian had a steeple crown with a brim that was turned up only on one side.

Hats of the 1870s were often made of crepe, silk, satin, felt, or velvet and trimmed with ostrich feathers and silk, satin, or velvet ribbons. Silver ornaments, such as buckles and brooches, were also quite popular as trimmings, as were high-backed filigree combs, which Victorian ladies sometimes used to artfully pin up one side of their hat brim.

LE MONITEUR DE LA MODE

A selection of fashionable hats from the early 1870s. (*Le Moniteur de la Mode*, 1873. Thomas J. Watson Library, Metropolitan Museum of Art)

For daywear, many fashionable ladies donned Neapolitan bonnets or bonnets made of Italian straw, split Belgian straw, or white or black chip. Some straw bonnets had hollowed out backs and brims that turned up in the front. Others were small and curved like an eighteenth century shepherdess hat. By the late 1870s, straw bonnets were being made to match a lady's ensemble. Formerly made in only one colour, they were now available in a rainbow of shades, from subdued hues of pale cream, drab, and silver to vivid tints of sky-blue, poppy-red, and mandarin.

Straw bonnets were generally trimmed with ribbons, flowers, gauze, or lace. Some had silk scarves tied around the crown and secured with a silver brooch or other ornament. In the late 1870s, straw bonnets could also be seen with braid trim or buttons of silver, gilt, or steel. Both hats and bonnets frequently had flirtatious ribbon streamers trailing down at the back. In England, these long, narrow ribbons which fluttered provocatively behind were popularly known as 'follow-me-lads'.[11]

Footwear: Elaborate Stockings, Button Boots, and Two-Toned Gaiters

By the 1870s, ladies' stockings had become even more luxurious and ornate. They came in a multitude of colours and materials. There were silk stockings and stockings of fine cashmere wool. For evening dress, many were woven in threads of silk and silver or embroidered with gold flowers. An 1876 edition of *Godey's Lady's Book* reports that gold butterflies could be found 'on the clocks of black silk stockings; small gold designs on red silk stockings; and anchors, worked in old silver, on navy blue stockings.'

Stockings were generally chosen to correspond with a lady's dress and shoes. They were available in plain and striped varieties, and in colours such as white, black, scarlet, blue, green, rose, and lilac.

For daywear, most fashionable ladies of the 1870s wore side-button boots made of French kid or pebbled leather. They came a few inches above the ankle and generally had pointed toes and Louis XV heels that were, at the beginning of the decade, about an inch and a quarter high. Ladies' boots were also available in styles which laced up at the front or side, as well as in more practical styles for walking which were made with wide soles and low, broad heels.

For evening dress, ladies wore button boots of white satin or kid which were often adorned with a rosette, ribbon, or other ornamentation at the toe. Silk and satin evening slippers were also quite popular, especially those with a low instep that served to showcase a lady's elaborately embroidered stockings.

Many ladies of the 1870s wore cloth gaiters over their boots. Gaiters attached with a strap under the instep and covered the ankle as well as the top of the boot or shoe. They came in several different colours and patterns, but grey, brown, or dark green were the most fashionable. Toward the end of the decade, checked patterns were also quite popular.

Outerwear: Casaques, Square-Cut Paletots, and Cambridge Jackets

For outerwear, ladies of the 1870s favoured jackets and *paletots*. The two terms were used almost interchangeably, depending on the ladies' magazine in which the garment was featured. According to the 1870 edition of the *World of Fashion*, there were three different styles of jacket or *paletot* which were 'equally fashionable for outdoor wear.' The first was the *Casaque*, which is described as:

> *'Fitting tight to the figure, and having the front part of skirt plain, and square in shape, while the back part is deeper, and is moderately bouffante in a great variety of forms.'*

The second most fashionable style of jacket or *paletot* was the short, square cut variety which had openings at the centre of the back and 'at the sides, extending nearly to the waist level'. The third most fashionable style had a longer skirt than the previous two and was worn open at the bottom of the back. It is described as being 'of medium width, slightly defining the waist but without fitting at all tight'.

Another popular jacket style of the early 1870s was the Cambridge Jacket or Cambridge Paletot. It was short, square, and double-breasted. A fashion plate in the 1872 edition of the *London and Paris Ladies' Magazine of Fashion* depicts a white

A short, square Cambridge jacket (centre) worn with a matching gown. (*London and Paris Ladies' Magazine of Fashion*, 1872)

cashmere Cambridge Jacket trimmed in blue velvet with long, open sleeves which were 'slightly rounded at the bottom'.

Jackets and *paletots* of the 1870s were often made *en suite* with a ladies' dress. They could also be made of cashmere or black silk trimmed in black lace or fringe.

Accessories: Long Gloves, Silk Parasols, and Oversize Fans

During the 1870s, gloves were worn for both day and evening. For daywear, they were made of kid, suede, or cloth and often fastened at the wrist with one or two delicate buttons. For eveningwear, the short puffed and elbow-length sleeves of 1870s dresses prompted ladies to begin wearing gloves that were elbow-length or longer. The August 1878 edition of *Myra's Journal of Dress and Fashion* reports that 'long gloves are a necessity with the half-sleeves now worn'.

Long evening gloves were generally made of silk or kid and fastened on the arm with rows of buttons. On some styles, there were as many as fifteen. Other long gloves were secured with buttons or snaps at the wrist. For those ladies who wished to show off their hands, fashion magazines of the day recommended mitts instead of gloves. According to *Myra's Journal of Dress and Fashion* 'the most fashionable mittens' were 'now made of lace, instead of netting'.

When outdoors, fashionable ladies of the 1870s were rarely without a stylish silk parasol. These parasols came in a dizzying array of sizes and colours. There were silk parasols trimmed with rows of lace; covered with white or black net, and edged with ruffles, bows, puffs, braid, or fringe. Parasol handles of delicately carved ivory, coral, and wood were equally dainty and ornate.

Though there were many varieties of parasol to choose from, the fashionable lady was advised to restrict herself to only those parasols which both complemented her dress and suited the occasion. The 1873 edition of *Cassell's Household Guide* states that silk parasols 'lined with white or pink' were acceptable for 'general carriage use'. For walking, parasols that were either 'perfectly plain' or 'surmounted with a couple of frills' were considered to be in the best taste. Parasol covers of black lace were also quite popular. They were economical as well. As *Cassell's* explains:

'A black lace parasol-cover is always a useful article, because it can be transferred from one parasol to another and makes it possible to wear for some time a light parasol which is a little soiled, or which has been cleaned.'

By the late 1870s, some ladies in visiting toilette were beginning to sport large parasols decorated with bouquets of flowers. The flowers were generally chosen to correspond with both the colours of a lady's dress and the flowers which trimmed her hat.

Fans were another fashionable accessory of the 1870s. They were generally quite large, often to the point of caricature. The 1873 edition of *Godey's Lady's*

A dress with matching silk parasol. (*Le Mode Illustre*, 1879. Thomas J. Watson Library, Metropolitan Museum of Art)

Book reports some measuring 'a yard length from tip to tip.' Fans came in a range of fabrics and colours, including brocaded silk and satin with sticks made of ivory or lacquered wood. Fans of hand-painted silk were considered to be the most beautiful of all. They were often worn suspended from a lady's waist by a chatelaine or a silken ribbon or tasselled cord.

Jewellery: Double Bracelets, Opera Chains, and Earrings of Every Type

Fashionable ladies of the 1870s often wore bracelets made of gold or silver filigree. They were especially fond of double bracelets. The 28 December 1870 edition of the *Morning Post* describes double bracelets as 'a pair of bracelets' that were worn 'one on each arm'. Double bracelets could be worn with long or short sleeves, but were generally placed on the arm 'over a tight sleeve or a long glove.'

Crosses and oval-shaped lockets suspended round the neck on slender chains, velvet ribbons, or silken cords were also fashionable in the 1870s. Some lockets featured enamelled crests or monograms. When made of silver or gold, they generally had a depressed centre and often featured an outside border of gemstones or pearls. Crosses could be made of silver, gold, or even diamonds. Some were made of rock crystal – a material which the 1871 edition of *Peterson's Magazine* reports as being 'much in vogue, especially for young ladies'.

One of the many novelties in jewellery of the 1870s was the long, opera chain on which a lady attached her watch. It was worn around the neck and, according to the 1871 edition of *Godey's Lady's Book*, had 'an adjustable slide" by which it could be 'fastened near the throat or lower down on the breast.' One end of the chain hung down below the line of a lady's belt. It was to this end that she attached her watch. The other end of the chain was short and finished with 'an ornately gold tassel.'

Perhaps the most popular item of jewellery in the 1870s was earrings. They came in a variety of styles which a lady could choose from according to her taste. There were gold and silver balls or clusters of pearls and gemstones suspended from delicate chains or wires. There were earrings of iridescent steel and earrings made in the shape of butterflies, bees, and beetles. For evening, many ladies wore earrings of diamonds or pearls.

Nature in Fashion: Butterflies, Stuffed Birds, and the Plumage Industry

Victorians had a fascination with natural history. This manifested itself in various ways, not the least of which was in fashionable clothing and décor. A Victorian parlour, for example, might feature a scientific display of pinned butterflies, while insects, such as butterflies, dragonflies, beetles, and grasshoppers, were often depicted in Victorian jewellery. Some insect brooches and hairpins were even set *en tremblant* (on a spring) so that the jewelled insect would tremble and shake as if it were actually alive.

Of these various insects, butterflies were undoubtedly the most well represented in Victorian fashion. During the 1870s, embroidered butterflies decorated women's ball gowns and stockings, enamelled butterfly pins adorned ladies' hats, and diamond butterfly hair ornaments accented fashionable coiffures. Ladies' magazines of the day also describe black satin shoes with butterfly bows made of jet and brilliantly coloured figured silks designed with butterflies, birds, and flowers.

Birds were also well represented in 1870s fashion. Though feathers of every variety had been fashionable throughout the Victorian era, it was not until the 1870s that ladies began to adorn their hats with actual stuffed birds, including doves, cockatoos, bluebirds, robins, and pigeons. The heads, tails, and wings of birds were also used for trimming hats and were often arranged amidst flowers and foliage to appear more natural. So many birds were used in fashionable dress that, during the nineteenth century, the plumage industry rose up to meet the demand. According to author Stephen Mosley in his book *The Environment in World History*, London soon became the centre of the international plumage trade, 'importing and re-exporting bird skins and feathers from the British Empire and elsewhere around the world'.

The craze for bird skins and feathers wrought havoc on bird populations and, by the end of the century, bird protection societies had formed in both England and the United States. Unfortunately, the fashion for hats ornamented with stuffed birds and exotic feathers showed no signs of dissipating. It would continue on, reaching its absolute height in the Edwardian Era, before at last fading away in the 1920s.

Chapter 5

The 1880s

'A lady can wear anything, yes— anything that becomes a lady, and every female of good taste may at the present time allow her good taste full scope without fear of "being out of fashion," whatever be the style of dress in which she chooses to appear.'
The *London and Paris Ladies' Magazine of Fashion,* 1885.

The 1880s ushered in an era of tailored, close-fitting gowns, some of which were almost masculine in appearance. These gowns exemplified women's changing roles in society. No longer content to be flounced, ruffled, and beribboned drawing room ornaments, ladies of the 1880s were engaged in outdoor pursuits. Some had jobs, some participated in sports, and many were involved in the ongoing fight for women's suffrage. This was the decade of Sherlock Holmes, Jack the Ripper, the Rational Dress Reform Movement, and the ready-made gown. This was also the decade when black evening dresses became fashionable – and not just for those in mourning.

The 1880s Silhouette

Beginning the decade, the general shape of ladies' gowns was similar to that at the end of the 1870s. The natural form was emphasized and bustles had fallen by the wayside, giving way to simple bum pads and elaborately draped fabric. For walking dresses, skirts were short and without a train. For afternoon and evening dresses, however, trains could still be quite long.

Both day dresses and dinner dresses were frequently made high at the throat with long, tight sleeves, sometimes decorated with a frilled cuff. For ball gowns, necklines were low and sleeves were often nothing more than a strap. Despite the emphasis on the natural form, waists at the beginning of the 1880s were still corseted, giving a lady's figure an hourglass shape which, in many cases, was not entirely her own.

Colours played a significant role in ladies' fashions of the early 1880s. An 1881 edition of the *Globe* reports that there was 'a decided inclination' for rich colours and that materials were 'fuller in tone, and of more decided hues'. At the same time, the aesthetic sensibilities of the decade were evinced in 'the blendings of various tints, or the combination of bright colours with neutral tints,' all of which are reported as being 'much more artistically and effectively managed'.

For day dresses and dinner dresses, there were shades of blue, sapphire, violet, green, crimson, ruby, and claret, while for evening dresses and ball gowns, shades of pale pink, such as blush rose or shrimp, were preferred. Most fashionable of all during the 1881 season were evening dresses and ball gowns in shades of white, which the *Globe* describes as being 'profusely trimmed with pearl or crystal beads and lace'. There were also black evening dresses which were trimmed with lace, beads, or jet and ball gowns trimmed with roses. Ladies of the early 1880s were especially partial to wearing a wreath or spray of roses on the bust and shoulders of their ball gowns. This configuration of flowers was called a *jardinière*.

Fabrics of the early 1880s were as rich and luxurious as their colours and trim. There were watered silks and satins, velvets and velveteens, India muslin embroidered with threads of silver and gold, and modernized seventeenth and eighteenth century brocades which, before the 1880s, 'were rarely seen otherwise than in museums, or in the wardrobes of ladies who had inherited them'.[12] In the colder months, gowns were often made of lush fabrics such as cashmere and brocaded velvet.

Patterned fabrics were also immensely popular, especially in day dresses. Ladies of the early 1880s wore plaid walking dresses with kilted underskirts or summer

A ball gown (left) trimmed with roses, similar to a Jardinière. (*Journal des Demoiselles*, 1880. Thomas J. Watson Library, Metropolitan Museum of Art)

frocks printed with dots of every variety. Addressing the enormous popularity of dots, the 1880 edition of *Godey's Lady's Book* states:

> *'Large dots, little dots, polka dots, Japanese dots, French dots, printed dots, brocaded dots, light dots, dark dots; dotted dresses, dotted mantles, plain fabrics trimmed with dotted ditto, and dotted fabrics trimmed with plain ones; dots of every style and of every size; dots for ever – such is Fashion's decree for this season.'*

In 1881, the Rational Dress Society was formed. It emphasized comfort and health in dress, as opposed to the unnatural and constrictive silhouettes of previous decades. Other dress reform organizations soon followed, but none could stop the eventual return of the bustle. It re-emerged in 1883, bigger and more dramatic than ever. This launched what is generally known as the second bustle period or second bustle era, which lasted from 1883 to 1889-90.

The increasing size of the bustle led to various changes in the structure of ladies' gowns, primarily in the draping of the skirts. They became straighter in the front and slimmer at the sides, devoid of any semblance of puffing or ruching at the hips. The entire focus of a woman's dress was now on the enormous bustle at the back, a protruding appendage upon which skirts and trimmings were heaped.

By 1885, the bustle had grown so large that, in many dresses, it appeared shelf-like. This led some Victorian fashion magazines to remind their readers that, though 'the tournure should lend itself to the figure,' it should never be the subject of 'independent swayings of its own'.[13] As the bustle gained in prominence, the front of ladies' gowns grew plainer. Tailored simplicity was the order of the day and, as an 1885 edition of the *London and Paris Ladies' Magazine of Fashion* declares:

> *'If you see a dress overloaded, either with drapery or trimmings, you may be sure that such artists as Worth or Felix have had neither head nor hand in its composition.'*

Skirts of the mid-1880s were gradually growing wider, with the fullness continuing to be arranged at the back. Some began to be attached to the bodice with gathers instead of pleats. These gathers were small at the front and very large at the back, creating a natural fullness which many fashion magazines hoped would decrease the size of the protruding, shelf-like bustle – or cause it to disappear altogether. As an 1885 edition of the *World of Fashion* explains:

> *'The fullness produced by the soft billows of a nicely-gathered skirt are much more satisfactory to the eye than the hard ungracious "bow-out" of the steel or horsehair appendage.'*

Trains of the mid-1880s were long, square, and narrow. They were still quite fashionable in evening dress, but they were now made separate from the skirts and could be worn or not worn depending on a lady's preference. Married ladies were generally expected to wear long trains and, according to the *World of Fashion*, young married women wore 'a modified form of train even for dancing'. Young, unmarried girls often dispensed with their trains entirely.

Bodices of the mid-1880s remained tight to the shape, but they were beginning to decrease in length. They now reached just below the waist, often coming to a distinct point. For day dresses, jacket bodices with short, standing band collars were all the rage. Sleeves were generally long and narrow, with elbow length or three-quarter length sleeves particularly popular in evening and dinner dresses.

When it came to fashionable trimmings, the mid-1880s was notable for silk fringe, cords, and tassels. Beading of jet, lead, bronze, and gold was also quite popular, as were lace, thread, and passementerie made entirely of steel. Many ladies of the mid-1880s accented their dresses with a belt or a sash. Belts were often paired with a jacket bodice. Sashes came in a variety of styles and could be worn either encircling the waist or 'laid as a drapery across the front' with long ends which fell to the edge of the skirt behind, terminating in two large bows.[14] Sashes were usually ten inches in width and, when worn around the waist, were made of soft fabrics, such as crepe or silk gauze.

Bustled gowns with standing band collars from 1885. (Thomas J. Watson Library, Metropolitan Museum of Art)

A VICTORIAN LADY'S GUIDE TO FASHION AND BEAUTY

As the decade progressed, ladies' day dresses became simpler and far more serviceable. They were generally made of plain or patterned wool, with the patterned variety sometimes interwoven with silk, satin, or gold and silver thread. Jacket bodices remained in fashion and waistcoats once again rose in popularity. Afternoon and dinner dresses were much more elaborate. They were sometimes embellished with lace or beading and bodices often featured an ornamental front called a plastron. Plastrons were typically made of silk, lace, or some other light material. According to the 1887 issue of *Godey's Lady's Book*:

> *'Plastrons are more fashionable than ever; the fronts of the bodices are either plain or plaited; they remain open shawl fashion to show the plastron, and are crossed over at the waist line. The plastron is either of silk or some fancy material that is also used in the trimming of the dress.'*

By the late 1880s, the draped overskirt was gradually beginning to disappear. In its place was a simple undraped skirt. This style was by no means universal, but it had a significant effect on the future of fashionable dress. As Cunnington explains:

> *'It also encouraged the open bodice and the loose-fitting blouse, and it gave the bustle its death-blow. Moreover it shortened the day skirt almost to the ankle.'*

For eveningwear, dresses were often both low-cut and sleeveless. This resulted in a scandalous expanse of naked flesh, leading an 1888 issue of *Godey's Lady's Book* to proclaim that 'no girl of ordinary discretion' would ever expose her bare arms and shoulders to view. Instead, if a lady's gown was made sleeveless and low across the bosom, *Godey's* advised that:

> *'She may employ for the neck a delicate lace tissue or tulle, drawn into fullness at the throat, and a half sleeve of the same material may be arranged to meet the long glove at the elbow. If the arm is thin, let the sleeve come below the elbow, as the effect is better than to draw the gloves up. Of all things, do not expose the sharp angle of the bone at the elbow.'*

As the decade came to a close, sleeves were growing fuller, a style which hearkened back to the romantic silhouettes of the 1830s. Bodices were fuller as well and were generally crossed in front on day dresses. No single style reigned supreme. Much was left to a lady's good taste and, as a result, styles of 1889 ranged from fashionable excess to stark simplicity. As the 1889 edition of *Woman's World Magazine* explains:

> *'There are two sides to current fashions, one characterised by great magnificence of material, the other as notable for extreme simplicity.'*

Undergarments: The Trouble with Bustles

In terms of undergarments, the 1880s is primarily remembered for the enormous size of ladies' bustles. Unlike the soft bustles of the 1870s, the more structured bustles of 1883-1889 were made of steel and springs with paddings of horsehair, down, or straw. They came in a variety of styles, including bustles that collapsed in on themselves when a lady sat down and bustles which were nothing more than cushions attached to a lady's corset.

At their largest size, bustles incited a fair amount of public criticism and ridicule. They were routinely satirized in magazines like *Punch* and featured as the subject of countless humorous – and not so humorous – newspaper articles. Many publications of the 1880s warned of the dangers posed by bustles. Just as in the era of the wire crinoline, there were apocryphal tales of steel bustles being struck by lightning or bustles which accidentally brushed into the fireplace and caused the bustle-wearer to burst into flames. Bustles were also blamed for a host of physical maladies, including everything from mere exhaustion to bad backs and deformity.

Some objections to the bustle had more to do with morality than health and well-being. For instance, in 1888 America, Captain Eric von Alexson of the Salvation Army received a letter of reprimand from his employers as a result of his wife's predilection for wearing a large bustle. The letter reads, in part:

'I do not think your wife in at all a condition to lead others away from the world and sin, and must say I am astonished to think you could uphold an officer, though she be your wife, in dressing herself in the manner Mrs. Alexson did. She was kindly reproved and shown the wrong, but persisted in wearing a bustle on her back that disgusted every decent person. Until I see her in sincere godliness I cannot send her to another station.'[15]

On occasion, ladies of the criminal classes used their large bustles to facilitate theft. Newspaper reports of the 1880s are rife with stories of bustles stuffed with all manner of ill-gotten goods, from clothing and jewellery to poultry and game. A few ladies even wore their stolen goods in the shape of a bustle in order to spirit them away from the scene of the crime. A notable example of this is the 1887 case of three British women who were arrested after police discovered that they were carrying twenty dead rabbits wrapped 'round their waists in the shape of dress improvers'.[16]

By the 1890s, the extreme bustle silhouette had fallen from favour. As a result, many tradesmen were left with a large stock of bustles and no way to dispose of them. In 1893, a draper in Melbourne resolved the issue by throwing his remaining stock of bustles into the sea, an action which prompted the *Sheffield Evening Telegraph* to humorously report that:

'Mermaids who have their abode in the sea round Melbourne are at present enabled to deck themselves out in the Parisian fashions of a bygone season.'

Millinery: Toques, Gainsborough Hats, and Flower Pots

Hats and bonnets of the 1880s came in a wide range of styles. One of the most fashionable varieties was the soft, brimless toque. There were cloth toques banded with velvet, sealskin toques edged with fur, and satin evening toques trimmed with feathers. Many Victorian ladies chose to have their toques made in fabric to match their gowns, a practice which the 24 April 1886 edition of the *North London News* describes as being not only inexpensive, but 'always fashionable and in good taste'.

In addition to toques, ladies of the 1880s were also partial to felt hats with large crowns, capotes with low brims, and close-fitting straw bonnets which tied beneath the chin with velvet ribbon bows. Some fashionable ladies wore square, high-crowned *directoire* hats with broad, flat brims that were turned up behind. Other ladies favoured the wide, bent brim of an elegant Gainsborough hat, an oversized style inspired by the hats worn by ladies in the eighteenth century paintings of Thomas Gainsborough.

By the middle of the decade, tall-crowned hats in the shape of flowerpots came into fashion. They had narrow brims and were often made of straw or silk plush. Upon their arrival on the Victorian fashion scene, one 1885 newspaper called them 'hat-trocious,' while another declared that they were 'one of the ugliest of the many

A selection of fashionable bonnets. (*Journal des Demoiselle* 1886. Thomas J. Watson Library, Metropolitan Museum of Art)

ugly hats that have been in vogue this year.'[17] Criticism notwithstanding, flower pot hats would remain all the rage for the remainder of the decade.

Hats and bonnets of the 1880s were notable for their trimmings. In addition to ribbons, feathers and flowers, ladies adorned their headwear with beetles, birds, butterflies, and fruits and vegetables. Many hats and bonnets were lined with shirred fabric or crepe. Others featured veils made of coloured tulle which were secured to the top of the crown and then drawn down over the face.

Footwear: Pointed Toes, Magpies, and High-Heeled Boots

Fashionable shoes of the 1880s were cut low in the instep, with pointed toes and curved heels that were sometimes as much as two inches in height. In the early part of the decade, ladies wore walking boots of 'fine black French kid stitched in white' and Moliére shoes made of black patent leather with high, Louis XV heels.[18] Button boots were sometimes trimmed with ribbon bows fastened at the top and shoes, like the Moliére, often featured large bows made of black faille.

By the mid-1880s, shoes adorned with bows and decorative buckles had fallen from favour. Instead, the most stylish shoes were plain, with no ornamentation at all save 'a very small satin bow or ribbon-tie'.[19] For evening, the 1885 edition of the *London and Paris Ladies' Magazine of Fashion* reports that shoes were 'worn as much as possible matching the dress, with white silk stockings'. If a lady's shoes did not match her dress, she was advised that her stockings should match her dress and that her shoes should be white.

Toward the end of the decade, shoes made of black patent leather and white buckskin were very much in fashion. Called 'magpies,' they were declared to be 'the smartest shoes' of the 1888 season.[20] Walking shoes with laces made in a corresponding colour were also quite fashionable, as were bronze evening slippers ornamented with beadwork or studs of cut steel, gold, or bronze. The mid-decade edict against lavish trimmings was discarded in favour of shoes adorned with rich embroidery, jewels – both real and paste – and buckles which were 'almost works of art'.[21]

A walking boot and a Moliere shoe. (*Godey's Lady's Book*, 1881)

Heels of the late 1880s were not generally as high as in previous years. They nevertheless fell in for their fair share of criticism. Many believed that high heels caused physical injury. They were thought to alter the natural line of the body, causing damage to internal organs, harming the spinal cord, and even exhausting the brain. As the 19 September 1889 edition of the *St. James's Gazette* explains: 'No woman who wore high heels had the full use of her life, nor of her brain possibilities'.

Outerwear: Pelisses, Mantelets, and Mother Hubbard Cloaks

There were many different styles of outwear in the 1880s. Most ladies wore coats, pelisses, or mantelets. Fashionable pelisses of the 1880s were usually full-length, with gathers at the shoulders and long, full sleeves. They were often made of velvet, silk, satin, or other rich materials. The 1884 edition of *Household Words* describes Parisian pelisses made of 'brocade, ottoman, stamped velvet, or silk and wool brocade'. These pelisses had 'modified jacket-sleeves' which were set high on the shoulder' and simple trimmings from neck to hem, including 'rich silk cord at the edge and knots of it on shoulders, at the waist behind, or looping across the front like a hussar jacket'.

A mother hubbard shoulder cape (left). (*Journal des Demoiselles*, 1881. Thomas J. Watson Library, Metropolitan Museum of Art)

Mantelets were also quite popular during the 1880s. They often took the form of a heavily trimmed short cloak which draped over a lady's shoulders. Some mantelets were longer, falling down over the arms to form sleeves. Others were fitted to the body, with peplums at the back which fanned out to accommodate the increasing size of a lady's bustle.

One of the most popular cold-weather garments of the 1880s was the Mother Hubbard Cloak. Available in a range of lengths, it was gauged at the shoulders with a high collar which tied at the throat. The 1881 edition of *Townsend's Monthly Selection of Parisian Costumes* calls the Mother Hubbard Cloak 'the most fashionable kind of covering for the coming season.' It was generally made in rich fabrics, such as brocaded satins and velvets, and trimmed with 'passementerie, rich lace, chenille, and heavy silk embroideries'.

Accessories: Satin Handbags, Feather Fans, and Twelve-Button Gloves

Most ladies of the Victorian era carried small, drawstring bags with them whenever they ventured outside of the house. These were the precursor of the modern-day handbag – petite receptacles for the various odds and ends a lady might need in the course of her daily travels. Depending on the occasion, they might hold anything, from paper money and coins to handkerchiefs, mint pastilles, and house keys.

In the 1880s, fashionable bags were often made of satin and velvet. The 1885 edition of the *Domestic Monthly* describes one style of bag fashioned out of garnet velvet and 'blue satin worked over with gold stars'. It was lined with 'gold-coloured satin' and finished with silk tassels and a drawstring of 'garnet satin ribbons'.

Feather fans were another fashionable accessory of the 1880s. They were generally made of ostrich feathers which had been dyed to match a lady's toilette. For those ladies who could not afford such a luxury, the *Domestic Monthly* reports that:

> 'A white ostrich fan is considered in good taste for all ball dresses, and a deep écru or tan-colored gauze, painted, with gilded or shell guards, is selected for ordinary evening wear.'

In addition to fans made of ostrich feathers, fans made of swansdown or peacock feathers were also quite popular. The 1885 edition of the *Art Interchange* describes 'cock feather' fans as being 'composed of long, silken feathers' which were 'daintily curled' at the tips. Feather fans of the 1880s came in a range of brilliant colours and, along with fans of painted paper and gauze, often featured sticks of tortoise-shell, ivory, or amber with monograms on the handles.

Gloves were, as ever, chief among a lady's fashionable accessories. In the 1880s, ladies preferred those made of soft kid, suede, jersey, or silk. For daywear, the *Domestic Monthly* reports that 'tan-coloured suede gloves remain without peer'.

Gloves made in shades of grey or light brown were also quite fashionable, especially when paired with a tailor-made dress. The stitching on the back of a kid glove was generally of a slightly deeper shade than the leather and, for streetwear, most suede and kid gloves fastened with four to six buttons at the wrist. Kid gloves with wide gauntlet or mousquetaire cuffs made of satin were also very popular, but these styles were not considered to be as flattering to a slender wrist and arm as a buttoned glove.

For evening, ladies of the 1880s wore long gloves made of light or cream-coloured kid which fastened tight on the arm with as many as ten or even twelve buttons. According to the 1881 edition of the *New Outlook*, 'the length of one's gloves in the present mode need only be limited by the length of one's purse and arms'. Long, buttonless gloves which were drawn loosely up over the arms were also considered to be very stylish. They had a slightly slouched, wrinkled appearance which the 1882 edition of *Godey's Lady's Book* describes as 'not tight-fitting all the way up, but rippling over the arm'.

In the summer, many ladies wore gloves made of silk or French lisle thread in shades of black, grey, tan, slate, and cream. Long, fingerless lace mitts were also quite popular. The *Domestic Monthly* describes 'pretty lace mitts, without fingers, with plain or fulled tops, open-worked, solid or decorated with silk embroidery'. Mitts were also worn for eveningwear, usually in shades of black, gold, or cream 'decorated with gold embroidery.'

Jewellery: Roman Intaglios, Ancient Coins, and Insect Pins

Jewellery of the 1880s was often prized as much for its originality as for its monetary value. Though many ladies still wore plain ball earrings or simple necklaces and bracelets for daywear, still others admired odd or eccentric pieces, some of which hearkened back to Roman or Byzantine times. In the mid-1880s, for example, Roman intaglios came into fashion. An intaglio was a gem or other piece of jewellery which had been cut with an incised or sunken design. Intaglios often took the form of large, decorative brooches, pins, or rings.

Ancient coins fashioned into jewellery were also quite popular in the 1880s. According to the 1885 edition of *Godey's Lady's Book*:

> *'Just now the rage of rages is for old battered coin converted into every imaginable sort of ornament, from hair and scarf pins, brooches and bracelets, bangles and buckles, and all that, to seals and buttons, and bits of fancy wear.'*

Ladies of the 1880s continued to wear pins and brooches constructed in the forms of butterflies, bees, beetles, and other insects. These could be made of gold or silver or comprised of precious jewels. Some insect pins were made true to scale. For instance, the 1884 edition of the *Jewelers' Circular and Horological Review* describes a small pin measuring 'about one inch in length' which was made 'entirely of gems and simulated a fly.' The fly's body was formed by two diamonds, one white and one green. The wings were 'composed of brilliants and two rubies formed the eyes'.

Gold bracelets remained a jewellery staple for both day and eveningwear; however, by the early 1880s, the fashion for double bracelets had fallen from favour. The 1 January 1881 edition of the *Tamworth Herald* reports:

> *'These jingling uncomfortable-looking circlets have given place to a more common-sense arrangement in the form of a single bangle bracelet that holds the long glove in place, and this, instead of being as loose as a bangle, is merely one slender band that clasps the arm tightly as a bracelet; but this mere line of gold often supports the richest gems.'*

The Aesthetic Movement: Art, Health, and Rational Dress

The Aesthetic Movement of the 1880s emphasized classical simplicity in dress. It was first associated with the Pre-Raphaelite painters, but later evolved into a sort of general 'bohemian counter-fashion' worn by creative people of every variety.[22] Those ladies who subscribed to the aesthetic philosophy, traded their bustles, corsets, and petticoats for loose, flowing dresses and tea gowns. These unstructured garments drew inspiration not only from classical styles, but also from the flowing elegance of the Japanese kimono. They were often made in soft silks, Asian-inspired prints, or fabrics which had been handwoven, embroidered, or coloured with soft, vegetable dyes. This was a stark difference from the dark colours and heavier, more upholstery-like fabrics and trim that were so much in fashion during much of the 1870s and 1880s.

Aesthetic dress received a mixed response from the Victorian public. Some found the loose, unstructured garments to be visually unappealing, while others felt that aesthetic dress bore too much resemblance to a dressing gown to be decently worn in public. Despite these concerns, the 23 June 1881 edition of the *Bath Chronicle and Weekly Gazette* admits that aesthetic dress 'does suit nine women out of ten, and is at any time more in accordance with common sense than a dress which looks like a bag tied above the ankles'.

By the end of the century, common sense in dress was becoming a matter of much greater concern. Women were working, attending college, participating in sports, or bicycling about town. They needed clothing which allowed for independence and freedom of movement. To that end, the Rational Dress Society emphasized a style of dress which would provide the 'the greatest possible comfort to the greatest number of wearers.'[23]

Proponents of rational dress claimed that tightly laced corsets, cumbersome dress improvers, and unwieldy crinolettes were injurious to a lady's health. At an

1883 meeting of the Rational Dress Society in London, the *Western Daily Press* reports that a woman named Mrs C. McLaren addressed the room, 'contending that the dress of women handicapped them in business and in domestic work, wasted time and health, and had no compensation in comfort or beauty'. The Rational Dress Society argued that dress should be secondary to the body and that, in order for women to be both healthy and productive, a 'perfect looseness of the dress throughout should be the first thing the society should insist upon.'

Japonisme: The Asian Influence on Victorian Fashion

In 1854, Japan opened trade with the West for the first time in more than 200 years. The influx of Japanese imports that followed inspired an intense fascination with Japanese art and culture. This fascination manifested itself in the paintings of Victorian era artists like Alfred Stevens, Vincent van Gogh, James McNeill Whistler, and Claude Monet. It also had a profound influence on Victorian fashion, helping to spur the transition from the heavy, multi-layered clothing of the 1860s to the sleek, streamlined silhouettes of the 1870s and 1880s.

In the late 1860s, the French term Japonisme (also known as Japonism) was coined to describe the influence of Japanese aesthetics on nineteenth century art and apparel in Europe and America. By the 1880s, Victorian ladies were quite noticeably beginning to incorporate Japanese elements into their dress. An 11 May 1888 edition of the *St. James's Gazette* reports that there was 'a decided tendency' toward Japonisme in every-day toilettes and that, though some years prior the Japanese had been praised for adopting French fashion, it was now to the East that French ladies looked for inspiration, thus 'setting themselves to the strange task of imitating their Oriental sisters'.

One of the biggest influences on late nineteenth century women's fashion was the Japanese kimono. Nineteenth century fashion magazines, newspapers, and society journals extolled its graceful lines and exotic, Eastern elegance. As an 1892 edition of *Table Talk* declares:

'Every fashionable hostess who will pour tea through the spring's sunny afternoons, will ache to possess a kimono after she has once noticed its graceful proportions setting off the figure of one of her sisters.'

Soon, kimono fabric and fabric with Japanese motifs, such as birds, fans, flowers, and fish, was being used to make dressing gowns and tea-gowns. *Table Talk* even went so far as to state:

'The interest recently taken in the costumes and social customs of our Oriental sisters is genuine; and, with various modifications, of course, it is

by no means improbable that our own and neighboring social circles may very soon be copying the Japanese modes with the same enthusiasm that for years has induced them to borrow ideas from the Parisian modistes and the London tailor establishments.'

By the close of the century, the popularity of the Japanese kimono had only increased. Though the sight of a Victorian woman wearing a kimono was still far from common, amongst the most fashionable society ladies, gowns made with kimono fabric or embellished with Japanese motifs remained all the rage. As one example, an 1898 issue of London's the *Sketch* reports on a 'smart' dinner party given by a society hostess in New York where all of the women in attendance wore Japanese kimonos.

Accompanying the article in the *Sketch* was the following humorous poem which addresses France's fading power over women's fashionable dress and the emerging influence of the Asian aesthetic:

*Good-bye to the time when the maid of our clime
Went over to France for the fashion,
And copied each craze (as the men did the plays—
Though wat'ring Parisian passion).
But now she is fanned in Chrysanthemum Land,
By taking its fashions on loan, O!
And changing her taste for the waist that is laced,
My lady adopts the kimono.*

*At first the Savoy gave her joy in the toy
When she ventured to see "The Mikado,"
And straight did succumb to the charm of Yum-Yum—
Though to copy her seemed like bravado.
But losing all fears with the flight of the years,
She does up her hair in a cone, O!
And now she can't stop, for she thinks she must flop
In the folds of a flowing kimono.*

*And if she'd begin to exhibit the pin
Which bonnets the sensible Jappy,
Instead of that vat of a matinée-hat,
I think I'd be perfectly happy.
For this aping Japan is a plan which a man
Must regard as pro publico bono
So I welcome the aid of the Japanese maid
In bringing the dragoned kimono.*

For the only drawbacks to this beautiful sack's
Replacing the corset and kirtle,
Is not in its hues, for our maidens can use
The shade of the delicate myrtle;
But our tongue makes it hard for the bard to discard
A rhyme which is compound in tone, O!
And thus it's a task for a jingler to ask
The Muses to rhyme to kimono.

The fashion for all things Japanese would continue into the twentieth century, lasting well into the 1920s and beyond.

The Dawn of the Black Evening Dress

The 1880s is also notable for being the decade when black evening dresses first came into fashion. They initially appeared in the ballrooms of France, but by 1881 they were being worn by British and American ladies as well. It was a dramatic shift from the lighter shades of fabric which had so far dominated women's evening dress. Not everyone approved of the change. Early in the decade, there were many who still viewed black as the colour of mourning – a fact which prompted one 1881 publication to declare that 'the prevalence of so mournful a colour gave a gloomy air to ballrooms' especially when the ballroom floors were 'stained to the hue of dark oak'.[24]

Despite the initial criticism, black evening dresses quickly became all the rage. Their popularity was attributed, at least in part, to the discovery that 'white shoulders' and a face that was 'flushed from dancing' looked far better 'in proximity to a black dress than to a white one.'[25] Not only were black evening dresses flattering to the complexion, they were also considered to be less expensive in the long-term. An article in the 3 May 1884 edition of the *North London News* describes them as being 'both fashionable and economical,' reasoning that black dresses showed their age less and were 'less quickly soiled' than light-coloured dresses.

To be considered truly stylish, ladies were advised that black evening dresses should be void of all coloured ribbons, flowers, or trim. Instead, the *North London News* states that black evening toilettes should be made in 'unrelieved black' and trimmed with jet. Fashionable black evening dresses were also often trimmed with steel or embroidered with lead beads.

Chapter 6

The 1890s

'The woman of fashion of to-day, if asked to express her feelings on the subject of attire, would say at once that it is the duty of women to look their best, and to contribute in this manner their quota to society.'

The *Woman's World*, 1890.

The 1890s ushered in an era of modest, dignified gowns, some of which were almost prudish in appearance. Necklines were high, skirts were straight, and enormous puffed sleeves contributed to an overall impression of women who were far more formidable than delicate. This was the decade of the New Woman, the Suffragette Movement, and the tailor-made dress. This was also the decade known as the Naughty Nineties in the United Kingdom and the Gay Nineties in the United States, a post-industrial period of decadence, wealth, and optimism.

The 1890s Silhouette

Beginning the decade, the tailor-made gown dominated women's fashionable dress. These gowns were comprised of jackets and skirts which were fairly masculine in appearance and, in many respects, not too dissimilar from a Victorian lady's riding habit. They were generally made in matched fabrics, such as wool, tweed, or flannel, and could be worn with a vest or a lady's high-necked blouse or shirtwaist. A shirtwaist was, quite simply, a tailored blouse or shirt with a collar and cuffs. Also known as 'waists,' they came in a variety of styles, including those made to look like a gentlemen's shirt or those covered with lace, frills, and embroidery.[26]

Fashionable dresses of the early 1890s were close fitting with fully lined, gored skirts which flared out into a bell shape and boned bodices which an 1890 edition of the *Woman's World* describes as fitting the figure 'like an outside skin'. At the same time, sleeves were gradually growing larger. Some styles puffed at the shoulders before gathering in at the elbows into a tight lower sleeve, while others ballooned out from shoulder to wrist in a fashion which hearkened back to the gigot or leg-o'-mutton sleeves of the 1830s. The *Woman's World* reports that on many fashionable gowns the sleeves were 'often made of velvet or silk, a shade deeper than the rest of the dress'.

The combination of puffed sleeves, tightly corseted bodice and bell-shaped skirts created a pronounced hourglass shape. This silhouette was often enhanced by the addition of a Swiss belt, corselet, or bands of ribbon. Swiss belts and corselets could be worn for both day and evening. Unlike traditional corsets, they were worn outside of the clothing to further emphasize the waist.

For evening, the flannels, wools, and tweeds of tailor-made day dresses gave way to softer, more delicate fabrics. Not only were silks and velvets quite fashionable, but the 1890 issue of *Godey's Lady's Book* reports that lace was coming into fashion again. For evening dress and ball gowns, there was even 'gemmed lace' – a version of lace wherein the pattern was outlined with precious stones, pearls, and diamonds. *Godey's* describes gemmed lace as being 'too rich and rare for ordinary wear.'

Though day dresses usually covered women's skin from neck to ankles, most evening dresses were cut low off the shoulder with round, square, or V-shaped necklines which dipped into a point in both the front and the back. Large, puffed sleeves were either elbow-length or short and were often adorned with ribbon bows. Bodices were rounded or slightly pointed at the waist and skirts were full, draping back into moderately sized trains. Trains and demi-trains were still a feature of both afternoon and evening dresses, but the popularity of longer trains was on the decline.

As the decade progressed, skirts of day dresses remained relatively plain and business-like. They were close fitting in the front and made fuller at the back with

A day dress worn with a Swiss belt (left). (*L'Art et la Mode*, 1891-1892. Thomas J. Watson Library, Metropolitan Museum of Art)

gathers or flat pleats. Bodices were usually much more heavily embellished, with styles that sometimes incorporated Elizabethan elements such as ruffs or padded sleeves. Puffed sleeves and wide lapels, known as revers, acted to broaden the shoulders. At the same time, skirts were gradually growing wider at the bottom where they were often stiffened with linen or buckram around the hem. This resulted in a silhouette that was even more distinctly hourglass.

In 1893, some tailor-made dresses began to be worn with an open coat over a plain skirt, shirt, Swiss belt, and necktie. This increasingly masculine style was combined with puffed gigot sleeves that were growing even larger and waistlines that were tinier than ever before. According to Cunnington, the average waist size in the early 1890s was 22 inches, but tight-lacing produced waists as small as 16 inches.

By 1895, sleeves had grown even larger and, in order to keep their shape, were often stuffed with eiderdown, stiffened muslin, or chamois. In some cases, internal sleeve support was provided by a wire hoop. Much like the gigot sleeves of the 1830s, the enormous sleeves of the mid-1890s fell in for their fair share of ridicule. Even *Punch* joined in, publishing a cartoon which depicted the latest novelties in sleeves, including sleeves shaped like hot air balloons and cricket bats.

For evening, fashionable dresses of the mid-1890s were usually cut square at the neck. Sleeves could be short, comprised of nothing more than a satin shoulder strap or a flounce of lace. Puffed, elbow-length sleeves were also quite fashionable. Gored skirts continued to cling closely to the hips. However, despite their sleek appearance, some skirts – especially those for evening – required a great deal of fabric. As the 1895 edition of *Godey's Lady's Book* reports:

> 'Some of the skirts are wide – very wide, according to our ideas. The most Parisian of cuts for an evening skirt at this moment demands fourteen breadths and fifteen seams; roughly speaking, the width around the hem measures about seven yards, but the cutting is so exquisite that it looks no whit wider when worn than an ordinary four-and-a-half-yard skirt.'

Evening dresses of the mid-1890s were made of rich velvets, silks, and satins in a variety of bright colours, including brilliant reds, emerald greens, magentas, violets, and yellows. Some evening dresses featured exquisite embroidery. Others were ornamented with lavish trimmings like jet or glass beads, braid, lace, rhinestones, jewels, sequins, and even iridescent steel spangles.

Sleeves reached their absolute largest in 1896. To the increasingly active woman, such bulk was insupportable. It is therefore somewhat unsurprising that, following the spring season of that year, both sleeves and skirts began to gradually shrink in size. Not only did skirts decrease in volume, they also began to grow shorter, with some as much as four inches off of the ground. Despite the rapidly reducing size of skirts and sleeves, the hourglass silhouette was still highly prized

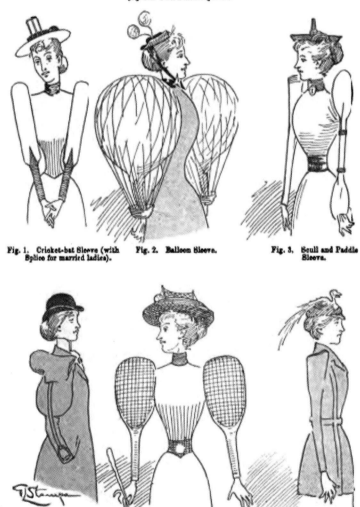

SUGGESTIONS FOR NOVELTIES IN SLEEVES.
(*By Our Own Fashion-plater.*)

Fig. 1. Cricket-bat Sleeve (with Splice for married ladies).

Fig. 2. Balloon Sleeve.

Fig. 3. Scull and Paddle Sleeve.

Fig. 4. Saddle sleeve.

Fig. 5. Racket Sleeve.

Fig. 6. Gun Sleeve.

A caricature of the fashion for puffed sleeves. (*Punch, Or the London Charivari*, 1895)

in women's dress. Swiss belts and corselets continued to be a fashionable option for emphasizing the waist.

As the century came to a close, the focus of fashionable gowns shifted from a lady's bodice down to her hips. To that end, a tight, hip-hugging skirt known as the eel skirt was introduced. It was made of gored sections at the front and the back and had a slight flare below the knees which fell all the way to the ground. It was not very practical for the active lady as it was quite difficult to move about in. However, the eel skirt did allow for a more subdued, feminine step. As the 6 April 1899 edition of the *Globe* reports:

> *'The hips and thighs are indeed closely fitted, but below the skirt springs outward, giving ample room, not only to step out but also to hold it daintily up at one side, which induces rather a pretty feminine attitude.'*

Day dresses of the late 1890s were made high at the throat with long, narrow sleeves which often extended down over the hand. For evening, gowns had square or rounded necklines and sleeves, if short, were little more than a strap. Skirts were full at the back, with fabric falling gracefully into double box pleats or accordion pleats. Waists were defined with sashes or bands of ribbon, but by 1899 the days of tight lacing were numbered.

A fashionable dress with a form-fitting, flared skirt similar to an eel skirt. (*Le Succes*, 1899. Thomas J. Watson Library, Metropolitan Museum of Art)

Undergarments: Eel Petticoats, Health Corsets, and Bust Bodices

Fashionable undergarments of the 1890s were made of fine fabrics with delicate trimmings. They were exceedingly feminine – and often exceptionally expensive. An 1895 edition of *Table Talk* describes ladies' undergarments that year as being nothing more than 'a series of cobwebby extravagance' comprised of 'linen of the finest, sheerest quality, trimmed profusely with costly lace'. *Table Talk* goes on to describe:

> *'Corsets of thick, brocaded silk, upon which the importer sets a fabulous price, and to match these, the strictly well-appareled woman must have petticoats of brocade—all this before the outerwear, in detail, is reached at all.'*

The 1890s fashion for close-fitting dresses and skirts necessitated undergarments which were equally sleek and close fitting. One such undergarment was the eel petticoat.

Made specifically for wearing beneath the hip and thigh-hugging eel skirt, the eel petticoat was short, with a deep flounce at the bottom. According to one 1899 report:

> '[Eel petticoats] are being made of glace silk, lined with flannelette as to the skirt, and stout muslin as to the flounce, which is often veiled with a flounce of lace or accordion-pleated brilliantine (a kind of cheap chiffon).'[27]

Corsets continued to be an essential component of dress in the 1890s, but rather than the unforgiving styles of corset from the previous decades, ladies now donned health corsets. Also known as swan bill corsets, health corsets were purported to put less pressure on a lady's vital organs. They were made with a straight busk and, when tightly laced, had the effect of forcing the torso forward and pushing the hips back. As a result, the bosom swelled into greater prominence.

The swelling, rounded mono-bosom which gave fashionable ladies the look of a pouter pigeon was further enhanced by a bust bodice which was worn over the corset. This sleeveless, lightly boned undergarment fitted over the arms with straps and laced closed at the centre front or back. The bust bodice is generally acknowledged as the forerunner of the twentieth century brassiere.

Millinery: Velvet, Tulle, and Doll-Crown Hats

By the 1890s, bonnets were no longer worn by any except the very elderly. Instead, fashionable ladies wore hats such as toques, brimless capotes, and straw hats with trimmings piled high on top to add height to a woman's frame. Hats were usually small to medium in size. The 1890 edition of the *Woman's World* describes cloth hats made in 'Edison blue' and brown velvet hats with rosettes placed above the forehead. There were also hats of Mandarin yellow velvet trimmed with brown ribbons and black velvet hats trimmed in jet.

In the mid-1890s, hats with very small crowns came into fashion. Known as 'Doll-Crown' hats, they featured a crown which the 17 August 1895 edition of the *Graphic* describes as being 'so small that it cannot possibly fit on any head.' Hats made of tulle were also considered quite fashionable, especially when made in white. As the 30 May 1896 edition of the *Graphic* reports:

> 'Nothing can be more effective than the masses of tulle lightly puffed about, with the most natural flowers nestling in the folds.'

The flowers of choice for trimming a tulle hat included white lilacs, white guilder roses, pale green poppies, and sprays of white honeysuckle. In addition to flowers, hats of the 1890s were trimmed with gold galons, feathers, or small pins adorned with miniature birds. As for the various animal welfare movements which sought to put an end to the plumage trade, the *Woman's World* states that:

'No crusade against the use of birds in millinery would seem to be of any use, for a great many are placed on every hat, not just one or a wing, as was the case a few seasons back.'

Footwear: Square Heels, Patent Leather Shoes, and Embroidered Evening Slippers

Fashionable ladies of the 1890s were far more active than they had been in previous decades. For long walks, golf, or other outdoors sports, they wore shoes of brown leather which either buttoned or laced. These outdoor shoes generally had long vamps and low, square heels, with some varieties coming up as far as the ankle. Practical boots and shoes of this sort are described as being 'quite extreme, and mannish in style' and were considered to be 'quite correct' when paired with the tailor-made costumes which were consistently worn throughout the decade.[28]

With more elaborate walking dresses, ladies wore shoes made of patent leather with broad soles and pointed toes that were sometimes adorned with a tiny buckle of gold or silver. They also favoured walking boots of black French kid or calfskin with the soles blackened in order to 'give more substance to the leather'.[29] For spring and summer daywear, ladies donned shoes and boots of white or grey doeskin. For evening, they generally wore dainty shoes or slippers made of satin or coloured kidskin. Evening shoes ornamented with steel, silver, or jet were also quite fashionable, as were slippers which featured embroidery or lace appliqué on the toes made to match the trimmings of a lady's evening dress or ball gown.

A selection of walking boots and shoes. (*Godey's Lady's Book*, 1895)

Outerwear: Velvet Cloaks, Short Jackets, and Feather Boas

The large, puffed sleeves of the 1890s often necessitated the use of sleeveless cloaks and capes as outerwear. The 1894 edition of *Godey's Lady's Book* describes short capes, some of which had 'stole ends' that reached 'half way down the skirt.' For older ladies and matrons, *Godey's* reports that these capes were sometimes made of 'black watered silk, trimmed with lace, net or accordion pleated chiffon'. They could also be seen in black moiré lined with 'black India silk' and trimmed with Chantilly lace and 'beaded jet passementerie'.

During the colder months, capes and cloaks made of velvet were considered the most fashionable. According to the 1895 edition of *Home Notes, London* 'there are few materials better than velvet for wearing when one wants to be warmly clad, and, at the same time, to have a really bright, smart-looking garment.'

Short or three-quarter length jackets were also quite popular. These were usually cut close to the figure and often featured short, stand up collars, puffed sleeves, and wide revers which *Home Notes, London* describes as turning 'back straight from the centre seam.'

Many ladies of the 1890s wore fur or feather boas wound round their throats. The 1892 edition of *Table Talk* reports that 'the newest feather boa, to twine becomingly about the throat with the afternoon tea costume' was made of 'white turkey plumes', while, dressier gowns were often paired with feather boas made of 'long white ostrich feathers, with black or seal-brown tips'. Feather boas were also available in bright colours, such as blue, green, violet, solferino (a vibrant, purplish pink), and magenta. When combined with a colourful dress, the effect could be quite garish, leading one publication to complain about 'the hideous mixtures of positive colours which have disgraced women all the spring'.[30]

By 1893, the fashion for long boas had fallen from favour, with some ladies' magazines even going so far as to state that 'to wear a long feather boa is to be hopelessly common'.[31] Instead, ladies were advised to keep their boas short, with the ends falling no further than just below the waist.

Accessories: Fan Bags, Giant Muffs, and Twenty-Button Gloves

Fans remained a fashionable accessory throughout the 1890s. When not in use, many ladies slipped their fan into a fan bag which they carried on their arm. Fan bags had once been a popular piece of fancy work which a lady who was skilled with a needle could make at home. By the 1890s, however, fan bags had become much more elaborate. According to the 1895 edition of *Table Talk*:

'Now it is an expensive article of trade. In old silver-and-blue (or pink) brocade, with its over-net chain, clasps, etc., of silver, it is not only lovely to behold, but costs "a pretty penny" also.'

Giant muffs were another popular accessory of the 1890s. They were generally made of fur, such as mink, sable, or beaver, but could also be found in rich brocades, feathers, and even in wolf skin. Unlike the fashionable muffs of the 1860s, fur muffs of the 1890s were enormous in size. They were worn suspended from the neck by a long, gold chain and were often made to match a lady's hat.

Fashionable gloves of the 1890s were not too dissimilar from those of the previous decade. Dark, one-button gloves made of suede or kid were all the rage for daywear, but only when worn with long sleeves terminating in cuffs that came down over the fingers. For wrist-length or shorter sleeves, ladies preferred long gloves.

For eveningwear, ladies wore gloves in delicate shades of white, grey, or cream which fastened on the arm with Roman pearls that were no larger than 'the size of a pea'.[32] Flesh-coloured gloves, such as those made in pale pink with rose-coloured pearl buttons, were also very popular. Some long evening gloves were secured with as many as twenty buttons. Others were worn long and wrinkled so that they appeared to slouch on the arm. The 1896 edition of *Godey's Lady's Book* reports that ball-gloves of this variety were often 'slashed at intervals and threaded with inch-wide ribbon of exactly the same shade, tied in a knot on the outside of the arm.'

Jewellery: Moonstones, Watch Wristlets, and Rings on Every Finger

Fashionable jewellery of the 1890s included brooches, rings, and bracelets set with moonstones. Moonstones were believed to have lucky attributes and were therefore a great favourite with the Victorian public. According to the 1890 edition of the *Woman's World*, they were 'much used for bangles' and could be found in brooches, which often took the shape of 'bars, stars, or safety-pins'. The most expensive pieces featured moonstones combined with diamonds or pearls.

Many ladies of the Victorian era wore small, jewelled watches pinned to their bodices. By the 1890s, some of these watches had been transferred to the wrist in the form of gold watch wristlets and bangles which were often enamelled or adorned with precious stones. Watch wristlets fell in and out of favour throughout the decade. For example, in 1891, *Godey's Lady's Book* reports that:

'Ladies do not seem to know what to do with their watches now. It is no longer fashionable to wear them in a bracelet, and it looks somewhat odd to see them hang at the neck like a locket, or pinned to the bodice like a

WATCH WRISTLETS AND BANGLES IN GOLD.

(By permission of Messrs. J. W. Benson.)

Bracelet watches, wristlets, and bangles were perfectly suited to the active women of the 1890s. (*Woman's World*, 1890)

soldier's medal. Then, again, dressmakers and tailors object to a watch-pocket in the bodice. So what is to be done with our watches if we do not wear a chatelaine?'

For active women—especially those who rode bicycles—wearing a watch attached to a chatelaine was not very practical. Bracelet watches made much more sense as they allowed a lady to check the time while keeping both hands firmly on the handlebars. When not bicycling, mid-1890s fashion magazines recommended that ladies don a corsage watch. These delicate time pieces were worn pinned to the bodice and are described as being 'as small as a five-cent piece'.[33]

Gold and silver rings set with turquoise, peridot, and other precious gems were another popular item of jewellery in the 1890s. Fashionable elderly ladies and matrons often wore glittering rings stacked on every finger; however, young ladies were advised to avoid excessive jewellery. As one 1894 publication explains:

'You who have the beauty of youth do not need to wear jewelry—a little ring, if you will, a modest brooch and perhaps a bangle on your wrist, but not an arm covered with them.'[34]

The New Woman

In 1894, author Sarah Grand published an essay in the *North American Review* titled 'The New Aspect of the Woman Question'. In her essay, Grand made reference to 'the new woman,' an intelligent female classed 'a little above' the common man, who was 'stronger and wiser' than her demure, feminine forebears. The phrase swiftly came to represent a stereotyped image of a modern woman who not only donned rational dress and rode a bicycle, but also insisted on gender equality – often to the point of parody.

Frequently accused of aping the mannerisms of a man, the New Woman was heaped with criticism, derision, and ridicule. *Punch* published satirical rhymes and cartoons and newspapers printed columns railing against the New Woman's ill manners, cleverness, and perceived lack of femininity. The *Gentlewoman*, a popular weekly paper for ladies, even went so far as to offer a prize to its readers for the best 'epigrammatic definition' of the New Woman. According to the 22 September 1894 edition of the *Surrey Mirror*, the winning submission described the New Woman as 'a fresh darn on the original blue stocking'. Other entries referred to her as:

> '"A creature of opinions decided and skirts divided," "One who has ceased to be a lady and has not yet attained to be a gentleman." "The unsexed section of the sex," "Man's newest and best reason for remaining single," "Madam become Adam."'

Such criticism did not quell women's desire for education, equality, and economic independence. By the end of the Victorian era, the New Woman had emerged as a feminist ideal. It would continue to be so well into the twentieth century.

PART II

Fashion Etiquette; or What to Wear and When to Wear It

Chapter 7

Victorian Ensembles for Every Occasion

'One of the great arts of dressing well is to know that what is appropriate to a morning négligé would be out of place in an afternoon, and would not do at all for the evening.'

Beeton's Young Englishwoman, 1875.

During the Victorian era, ladies of the middle and upper classes changed their gowns multiple times each day. There were morning dresses, walking dresses, visiting dresses, and evening gowns – to name just a few – each suited for a particular time of day and a particular setting. The fashionable Victorian lady was well aware of these subtle differentiations and would no more wear a morning dress to dinner than a nightgown to a ball. At the bare minimum, her wardrobe comprised dresses which were suitable for morning, afternoon, and evening. In the later Victorian era, walking dresses and dinner dresses would also be essential.

Morning Dress

A Victorian lady's first change of clothes of the day was out of her wrapper or dressing gown and into a morning dress. A morning dress was an 'at home' gown of simple design. It usually had long sleeves, a high neckline, and minimal trimming. A lady might wear a morning dress to meet with her housekeeper or cook or to receive morning calls from her close friends.

Morning dress hems were generally short, just touching the floor. During the 1870s and 1880s, 'moderate trains' were fairly common.[35] In her 1999 book, *Authentic Victorian Fashion Patterns*, Kristina Harris specifies the precise length of skirts and trains on morning dresses, writing:

'The dress hem could be short, but often touched the floor in front and at the sides, with a train no longer than six inches in the back.'

Though morning dresses were meant to be relatively comfortable costumes for at home, they could still be quite structured. Their shape mirrored the popular shape of the decade, whether that be the enormous skirts of the 1850s and 1860s or the slim fitting silhouette of the 1870s and 1880s. In the late Victorian era, for example, many ladies donned tea-gowns which could be worn without a corset for at home wear.

Walking Dress

By the 1860s, walking dresses had emerged as a style distinct from that of the ordinary afternoon dress. They had shorter skirts, allowing for ease of motion, and were often worn by fashionable ladies for strolls in the park or shopping trips into town. Most walking dresses were made without a train; however, by the 1870s and 1880s, some possessed skirts which brushed the ground in front and were trained or artfully draped at the back. The 1885 edition of the *World of Fashion* describes one such style of walking dress with skirts that were 'arranged with a bouffant and waterfall drapery' behind. For walks, trained skirts could easily be drawn back and 'passed through a loop at the waist' to get them out of the way.[36]

Walking dresses were usually made of richer fabrics than morning dresses. In addition to cotton, mohair, and merino wool, they could be found in richly coloured silks, satins, and cashmere. Ladies' magazines of the day describe fashionable

A morning walking costume made of brown cashmere. (*Ladies' Monthly Magazine*, 1876)

walking dresses made in shades of maize, apricot, pearl-grey, and violet. However, in *The Ladies Manual*, published in 1883, I.N. Reed advises that, for walking costume, 'black is the most becoming colour for street dress'.

The illustration at left shows a fashionable, brown cashmere and wool walking dress from the 1876 edition of *The Ladies' Monthly Magazine*. It is described as follows:

> *'MORNING WALKING COSTUME. Fig. 1. — Dress à deux jupes and tight-fitting Paletot en suite. The under-skirt is of brown cashmire. At the bottom is a flounce headed by a biais band of checked woollen material of a light olive brown shade; having a frill at each side. The upper-skirt and Paletot are of the light olive brown checked material. The front of skirt forms a draped tablier. The sides are caught up and finished by frills and bows, the back is slightly bouffante and forms a long point. The front of Paletot is deeper than the back, and it closes by buttons. The top is finished by a deep collar, and the sleeves have cuffs; the collar and cuffs, with the bottom edges of the Paletot and upper skirt are finished by bonds of the plain cashmire. Chapeau of brown terry velvet, with white lace and feathers.'*

Afternoon Dress

Afternoon and visiting dresses were more elaborate than either morning or walking dresses. Skirts were trained and necklines could be lower. They were worn for receiving visitors at home or for paying calls. The formality of these dresses could differ widely since much depended on the rank of the person on whom the lady was paying her afternoon call. The more distinguished the personage, the more luxurious the visiting dress.

In addition to being more heavily trimmed than morning dresses and walking dresses, visiting dresses were often richer in both fabric and in colour. During the 1870s and 1880s, they were generally trained. However, if one was paying a call on foot (as opposed to by carriage), etiquette manuals strongly advised against long skirts and a train. As *Beeton's Young Englishwoman* explains, 'nothing is more ridiculous or much dirtier, to speak plainly, than a long dress in the street'.

Dinner Dress

A dinner dress was more formal than an afternoon or visiting dress, but not as elaborate as an evening gown. According to Harris, the skirts touched the floor all the way around and, usually, featured a train of 'up to ten inches'. Dinner dresses often had elbow length sleeves. Necklines could be low; however, by the mid-1870s and into the 1880s, the most fashionable dinner dresses had high necks.

Shown from left to right, a walking dress, dinner dress, evening dress, house dress, and visiting dress. (*Godey's Lady's Book*, August 1875)

Victorian dinner dresses were usually made in rich, shimmering fabrics like silk brocade, satin, or velvet and were often trimmed with glass beads, jet, lace, or even flowers.

Evening Dress or Ball Gown

An evening dress or ball gown was the most splendid garment of a Victorian lady's wardrobe. Sleeves were usually short and trains were as much as 65 inches in length. Fabrics and trimmings varied according to taste. For 1875, *Beeton's Young Englishwoman* advises:

> *'If made of light materials, evening dresses, as a rule, are very elaborately trimmed; but if heavy fabrics are selected, they can be made up simply, if preferred.'*

For dancing, long trains could be pinned up. Alternately, some Victorian dancing masters advised that ball gowns be made without a train.

Chapter 8

Victorian Riding Habits

'It has often been observed that a lady never appears to greater advantage than when she is tastefully habited and mounted upon a handsome horse.'

The *Columbian Lady's and Gentleman's Magazine,* 1846.

Riding habits of the Victorian era were both fashionable and functional. They were designed to flatter the figure, camouflage the dirt, and withstand the physical rigors of horseback riding. These basic, practical considerations did not change a great deal from season to season – or decade to decade. As a result, the favoured fabrics, cuts, and colours of riding habits at the end of the Victorian era were not dramatically different from those at the beginning. This was especially true in the early Victorian era. As an 1842 issue of *The Lady's Companion* explains:

'While carriage and walking-dresses are continually changing in fashion, there occurs but little or no variation in the style of riding habits.'

This does not mean that every Victorian riding habit was identical. There were, in fact, significant changes in the cut of the habit bodice over the century, as well as in the preferred styles of sleeves, buttons, trimmings, and hats. Nevertheless, according to *The Lady's Companion*, styles in riding habits from the 1830s to the 1840s underwent no material change. In both decades, the habit bodice could be worn 'buttoned up to the throat,' 'left half open at the chest,' or 'thrown entirely open to display a smart and handsome vest'. Meanwhile, skirts remained long and full, reaching well below the feet.

As for the colour, *The Lady's Companion* states that 'to be in good taste,' the colour of a lady's habit should 'never be light'. Dark colours were much more acceptable, with shades of black, deep blue, and dark green predominating throughout the era.

No matter the colour, fashion magazines of the early Victorian era declared that the collar of a riding habit must be made in velvet. The cuffs were often velvet as well. The habit itself was generally made of fine cloth and the best varieties were cut and sewn not by a seamstress, but by a gentlemen's tailor. For those habits worn with a vest, ladies were advised that the vest should be buff or light blue and that

A typical riding habit
of the early 1850s.
(*Le Moniteur de la
Mode*, 1853. Thomas
J. Watson Library,
Metropolitan Museum
of Art)

'small shirt-collars with some showy colour' were more becoming than fine lace.
Even the buttons of a lady's riding habit were a subject deserving of attention. As
the *Lady's Companion* reports:

> *'Purple and green habits should be trimmed with stuff buttons; but blue
> habits should always be ornamented with small gilt buttons, very rich in
> luster, perfectly plain on the surface, and set closely together in the rows.
> These buttons are always worn on the vest, when the bodice is thrown open.'*

Riding habits of the mid- to late-Victorian era frequently featured velvet collars
and cuffs as well, though later styles did admit to some variation. Riding habits of
the 1860s, for example, often had loose-fitting sleeves with wide, gauntlet cuffs.
Conversely, an 1878 edition of the *Gentleman's Magazine of Fashion and Costumes
de Paris et Londres* describes a lady's riding costume made with cuffless sleeves
which were trimmed at the wrist with 'buttons and short tabs of velvet'.

As a general rule, riding habits were made with tight bodices, close sleeves, and
full skirts. Some habits of the 1860s had basque bodices, which extended down
past the waist at the back. Others were made short, either all around or just at the
front. An 1863 edition of *Godey's Lady's Book* describes one such style of bodice,
which was made 'very short in the waist' in order to show the white cashmere vest
worn beneath.

Habit bodices of the 1870s and 1880s were made without basques. Instead, they
are reported as having 'merely the coat-tail at the back'.[37] Some were made open at the
throat to reveal a light-coloured scarf tie. Others were made open either at the waist

A riding habit bodice with a short jacket. (*Godey's Lady's Book*, 1863. Accessible Archives)

or at the chest in order to display a fancy, patterned waistcoat beneath. In her 1887 book *Riding for Ladies*, Mrs Power O'Donoghue expresses her disapproval of the 'startling' colours and designs of some of these waistcoats, advising her readers that:

'The nicest shaped bodice for a lady is one made closely buttoned up, almost to the throat, showing merely a small linen collar above the braid or neck-band, with the addition of a neat tie of no conspicuous colour. The bodice itself should be entirely free from ornament of any sort whatever.'

Beneath the skirts of a riding habit, Victorian ladies wore riding trousers made of either cloth or a combination of cloth and chamois leather. According to an 1884 issue of the *Clothier and Furnisher*, the best-fitting riding trousers were sewn by tailors who had, in the back of their shops, 'a wooden horse on which the ladies sit while their cloth skirts are draped to hang well over the tight fitting pants'. In the 1890s, ladies discarded their riding trousers, choosing to wear sturdy knit tights beneath their habits instead. As an 1894 edition of *Good Housekeeping* reports:

'The best equipped horsewomen universally use jersey tights either black or the colour of their costume, and do not order a pair of trousers made to match the materials of their habit, as they once did.'

By the late Victorian era, many ladies were beginning to don safety skirts with their riding habits. Invented in 1875, a safety skirt was made with either buttons or special stitching at the seams which was designed to give way under pressure. Before the invention of the safety skirt, if a lady's skirts caught on the pommel of her side-saddle during a fall, she might be dragged along behind her horse as it galloped away. Some unfortunate Victorian ladies were killed in riding accidents when their skirts caught on their saddles. With the safety skirt, however, the 'burstable seams' would simply burst, freeing the lady from her horse before she suffered serious injury.

VICTORIAN RIDING HABITS

The practicality of safety skirts did nothing to diminish the elegance of ladies' riding habits. As the decades progressed, they continued to be recognizable for the quality of their fabric and the perfection of their tailoring. Simplicity remained the last word in riding costumes well into the 1880s and 1890s. Any efforts to decorate the habit with an excess of feathers or a tasteless display of trim was frowned upon by both Victorian fashion magazines and equestrian manuals alike. As one 1884 equestrian manual explains:

> *'A riding habit should be distinguished by its perfect simplicity. All attempts at display, such as feathers, ribbons, glaring gilt buttons, and sparkling jet, should be carefully avoided, and the dress should be noticeable only for the fineness of its material and the elegance of its fit.'*[38]

When riding, Victorian ladies always wore a fashionable riding hat or bonnet. Riding hats were expected to be both sensible and in good taste. In the early Victorian era, for example, a neat cap of velvet or cloth equipped with a veil was preferable to a Leghorn or cottage bonnet which might prove troublesome by flapping about in a high wind. From the 1850s to the mid-1860s, the *Woman's World* magazine reports that 'low crowned hats with flowing plumes seem to have been almost universally worn'. While at the end of the Victorian era, most ladies preferred high-crowned hats of black beaver or felt, complete with long veils made of fine, silk gauze.

A ladies riding habit worn with a high-crowned beaver hat. (*Gentleman's Magazine of Fashion,* 1876)

Riding gloves were another necessary accessory for the Victorian equestrienne. They were a purely practical item, with worsted gloves being superior to those made of kid. Kid gloves were known to chafe on the reins. Equally practical were the plain, leather boots that ladies wore when riding. Unlike walking boots, they were made without high heels, buttons, or other fancy embellishments that could get caught on the stirrup. Instead, they were made in a similar fashion to a gentlemen's hunting boot, with low, broad heels and a flat upper which allowed for a lady to obtain 'a firm level bearing on the stirrup-iron'.[39]

By the end of the century, solid, plain cloth riding habits had given way to coloured waistcoats and a variety of hats ranging from 'the round felt and the soft wide-awake to the jaunty little sailor hat for summer mornings'. As *The Woman's World* magazine reports:

> *'Everything, indeed, tends to a rational form of riding-dress. Habits are not so short as they were last year, neither is it considered necessary to exhibit an "hour-glass" waist in the saddle, while the form of head-covering is left widely to the fair rider's taste.'*

The drift toward greater functionality and freedom of personal expression in riding habits was reflective of changing public views, not just of women, but also of exercise and athletics. Accomplished equestriennes were beginning to be appreciated as much for their skill in the saddle as for the cut of their coat. Of course, an elegant riding habit must always be admired, but as the nineteenth century drew to a close, no longer could it be said of the female equestrian that 'graceful as may be the style of her riding, there is little that is interesting in her appearance unless she is properly attired'.[40]

Plain cloth riding habits in neutral colours remained in fashion throughout the Victorian era. Riding Habits, Freja: *Illustrerad Skandinavisk Modetidning,* 1889. Nordic Museum, Sweden)

Chapter 9

Holiday Fashion

'The close of the London and Parisian Season has now arrived, and the Fashionable World has sought the invigorating breezes of the Seaside...'
The *Ladies' Monthly Magazine*, 1869.

During the Victorian era, there was no such thing as a holiday from fashion. Seaside resorts in England – whether in Brighton, Bournemouth, or Burnham-on-Sea – were as much a place to flaunt one's style as London itself during the season. An 1869 issue of the *Ladies' Monthly Magazine* even goes so far as to declare:

'Splendid as they have been in the season just ended, dresses to be worn at the Seaside, and at the mansions of our Aristocracy, often surpass those that have been worn in London or Paris, during the height of the Season.'

Seaside Dresses and Accessories

In the early Victorian era, seaside dresses were often quite similar to walking dresses. They were made in light fabrics and worn with straw hats and veils that covered part or the whole of the face from the sun. It was not until the 1860s that a definitive 'seaside costume' began to emerge. A seaside costume was differentiated from other garments primarily by its fabric and ease of fit.

The 1862 issue of *Godey's Lady's Book* reports that 'quilting dresses' were very much in style for the seaside that season. These dresses were either plain white, striped, or 'sprinkled over with field flowers.' Cotton piqués were also extremely fashionable resort wear, especially in buff, mauve, white, and 'tea-coloured.' These dresses often comprised a skirt and a jacket and were trimmed with red, white, or black braiding.

The enormous skirts that were so fashionable in the 1860s were not entirely practical for seaside wear, especially if one intended to walk on the beach. The 1864 edition of the *Englishwoman's Domestic Magazine* reports that, at the beach, full skirts were worn 'looped up' to keep them out of the way. They were often paired with boots with 'tops heart-shaped in the centre' from which descended a small, ornamental tassel. Boots made of Russian leather were considered to be

Seaside costumes were often comprised of a skirt and a jacket trimmed with braid. (Beilage zur Victoria, July 1863. Thomas J. Watson Library, Metropolitan Museum of Art)

'particularly suitable' for those places where the sand was 'fine and abundant,' but ladies could also be seen wearing 'small high-heeled shoes' with gaiters made of 'white or unbleached linen.' As the *Englishwoman's Domestic Magazine* explains, 'An elegant boot is essential now that feet are so much seen.'

By the late 1860s, the silhouette of ladies' gowns was beginning to change. Fabric that had once been draped over enormous wire crinolines was now being drawn to the back and draped over a bustle. Seaside costumes were not immune to this metamorphosis. Still, seaside gowns managed to remain distinguishable from morning gowns, walking gowns, and other dresses mainly by virtue of the fabric used – cotton piqués, cashmere, or wool – and the simplicity of their trimmings.

Seaside costumes of the 1870s remained fairly similar in shape to the walking dresses worn during the season. In prints, fabrics, and trimmings, however, seaside fashion was sometimes whimsical. For example, an illustration in the 1870 issue of the *Milliner and Dressmaker and Warehouseman's Gazette,* depicts a seaside dress made of silk covered with 'sprays of poppies and ears of corn'. The lady is also wearing a hat trimmed with 'wheat-ears'. The full description reads:

'Dress of white foulard silk, covered with sprays of poppies and ears of corn. The train-skirt has a gathered flounce, headed by a high marquise ruche, edged by maize-coloured silk. A tunic bodice, with revers in front of the bodice and skirt, bordered by a pleating of maize silk. A double row of silk

96

Whimsical seaside costumes patterned with ears of corn. (*Milliner and Dressmaker and Warehouseman's Gazette* 1870)

> *forms the sash. Sleeves with revers, trimmed with a pleating of maize silk. Rice-straw hat raised at the back, trimmed with a bow of red ribbon, a tuft of feathers and wheat-ears.'*

The skirts of seaside dresses were usually shorter – with a hemline at or above the ankle – for ease of movement. In 1877, some seaside dresses were beginning to be made with a fabric called seaside barège. According to *Godey's Lady's Book*, this soft, white wool fabric resembled flannel, but was of less weight and 'cool as muslin.' As *Godey's* states:

> *'[This fabric promises] to be very extensively used for country toilets, especially at the seaside, where the moisture takes the starch out of cottons and linen.'*

The availability of more beach-friendly fabrics did not affect the popularity of cotton, which continued to be used for seaside costumes throughout the Victorian era. Fine batistes and lawns in delicate colours and stripes were also well represented at the seaside, as were linens and woollens. Some ladies of the 1870s are even reported as wearing seaside costumes made entirely of Spanish lace.

By the end of the 1880s, seaside costumes were tighter and narrower than ever. An 1888 edition of the *Woman's World Magazine* describes them as 'sheath-like seaside costumes that cling to the figure' like an 'outer skin'. These tight-fitting seaside dresses gave way to the popular middy blouses (blouses with a sailor collar) and flared skirts of the 1890s.

A lace seaside costume with lace-trimmed parasol. (*Freja: Illustrerad Skandinavisk Modetidning*, 1882. Nordic Museum, Sweden)

While on summer holiday, ladies accessorized their fashionable seaside dresses with hats and parasols. These varied in style throughout the Victorian era; however, as a rule, straw hats were generally preferred for beachwear. At the end of the century, some ladies began to wear duck or linen sailor hats which were made to match their gowns. Sailor hats were frequently trimmed with a band of ribbon which matched a lady's belt or neck scarf. Parasols could also be made to match a lady's dress, but some ladies preferred parasols in a contrasting colour.

The close of the Victorian era saw record numbers of people spending their holidays at the beach; not only the fashionable upper classes, but the working classes, too. In fact, according to a 1900 issue of the *Speaker*:

'We believe it would be found on a careful estimate that there are more people in the seaside holiday places of southern England than in all the other seaside places of the world put together.'

With so many people drawn to the seaside each year, it is no wonder that seaside costumes became a subject of paramount importance for ladies on summer holiday. Whether at a public beach or a quiet watering place, for the well-to-do Victorian lady, there truly never was a holiday from fashion.

Bathing Costumes

When visiting the seaside, many Victorian ladies enjoyed a dip in the water. This necessitated the donning of a bathing costume and, generally, the use of a bathing machine. Victorian bathing machines were small, roofed wooden cabanas used by bathers to change out of their street clothes and into their bathing costumes. The bathing machine was then wheeled out into the sea where the now suitably clad occupant could disembark by means of steps which led down into the water. For ladies, these steps were often concealed by an umbrella, a canvas hood, or other covering which shielded them from view until they were safely—and modestly—submerged beneath the waves.

In the early Victorian era through the 1870s, bathing costumes generally consisted of a dark-coloured tunic and trousers made of serge, alpaca, or heavy flannel. It some respects it was not too dissimilar from the Bloomer costume of the 1850s. The trousers were long and full, coming down to fasten at the ankles with a button. The tunics had long or elbow-length sleeves and were sometimes tailored or belted at the waist to give a bit of shape to an otherwise shapeless ensemble. Lace-up bathing slippers and an oilskin cap or wide-brimmed straw hat completed the picture.

Victorian bathing costumes were considered to be rather remarkable for their ugliness. An 1855 edition of *Graham's American Monthly Magazine* states quite

A woman in a bathing costume descends into the sea. (Coloured lithograph by A. A. Bonnaffé, after Jules Gaildrau, (1816-1898). Wellcome Library, London. Creative Commons Attribution 4.0 International Public License)

firmly that 'there is no becoming bathing costume – it is useless to seek it', while a comic verse in an 1854 edition of *Bizarre* asks its readers:

'*Who ever lost his heart for a woman in a bathing dress? We won't pause for a reply: we hear it on every side, "No one, nobody."*'

Even the fashionable French had yet to come up with an attractive style of bathing costume, leading an 1852 edition of the *Ladies' Companion and Monthly Magazine* to opine that:

'*It must require some courage to doff their pretty gowns, graceful mantelets, and becoming little bonnets, and emerge from the tent where they change their attire, in the oil-skin cap, the tunic and trowsers, and list slippers.*'

By the late Victorian era, bathing costumes had improved a little in appearance from the shapeless, sagging ensembles of the earlier part of the century. Sleeves were now short and puffed, baring a lady's arms. Trousers were shorter as well, now reaching just below the knee. In addition, the late-1860s invention of the bathing corset, which was fashioned from whalebone and made to wear beneath one's bathing costume, helped ladies to keep their fashionable shape in the water. A less constrictive means of support popularly known as 'bathing stays' soon followed. As one 1877 magazine states:

'*An enterprising firm has just patented some bathing-stays, which Frenchwomen much appreciate, whether for swimming or merely plunging in the water, for they support the figure without interfering with their ease of movement.*'[41]

Despite some advances in style, Victorian bathing costumes were still a trial for many ladies of the late nineteenth century. Wet fabric clung to the body, revealing details – and defects – of a lady's figure which she would never dream of revealing outside of the water. To combat this less than flattering picture, ladies were advised to wear stripes if they were too stout and long sleeves and stockings if they were too lean. They were told which fabrics were best for salt-water (cotton), freshwater (wool), and swimming (silk), and warned never to wear light coloured bathing costumes with a yellow tinge lest, when wet and clinging, they appeared 'too nearly the colour of skin'.[42] Indeed, according to one 1890 publication, a lady never presented herself 'under more trying circumstances' than when 'preparing for a dip' in the ocean.[43]

Chapter 10

Victorian Sportswear

'As a nation we ought to welcome the healthy, hearty girl who can beat her brother in managing a tennis ball, in rowing a boat, and very often in managing a frisky horse.'

Ladies Home Journal, 1891.

Throughout much of the Victorian era, a woman's role in relation to athletics was more that of spectator than participant. Clad in restrictive undergarments and bulky gowns, fashionable ladies stood on the sidelines and watched as men took part in both competitive sports and informal games. Ladies who wished to participate in outdoor play were relegated to croquet, a game which has been unflatteringly described as being comprised of nothing more than 'frills and fancies, of petticoats, giggles and maidenly blushes'.[44]

By the 1870s, many ladies were beginning to desire more than just a decorative game of croquet. They began to participate in more competitive sports, such as lawn tennis and golf. They also began to ride bicycles, both for pleasure and as a means of transportation. These various athletic endeavours necessitated that women's clothing be adapted to suit. Such changes did not come quickly and, in some cases, were not wholly satisfactory when they did arrive. Nevertheless, ladies of the late Victorian era – however unsuitable their dress – not only managed to participate in competitive play, some of them even went on to make sporting history.

Lawn Tennis

The game of lawn tennis was invented in the 1860s by retired British army officer Major Walter Clopton Wingfield. He patented the game in 1874 and, within a few short years, lawn tennis had become one of the most popular sports for women in Victorian England. Ladies played it at society garden parties and at tennis clubs. By the mid-1880s, they were even competing at Wimbledon, leading the 1891 edition of the *Wright & Ditson Officially Adopted Lawn Tennis Guide* to declare that:

'Lawn tennis has done more to develop among girls a taste for outdoor sports than have all other exercises combined.'

A VICTORIAN LADY'S GUIDE TO FASHION AND BEAUTY

Initially, an excess of athleticism was not encouraged in women. In fact, in her 2010 book *The Sporting Life*, Nancy Fix Anderson explains that, though lawn tennis required a certain degree of physical exertion and strength, Victorian ladies were discouraged from playing in a competitive manner. Instead, they were urged to simply hit the ball to their opponent. In similar fashion, the *Lawn Tennis Guide* downplays women's athletic ability, praising instead 'the charm women bring to tennis'. As the guide states:

> *'They are graceful and gentle; they have spirit and enthusiasm; and in tennis, as in other things, they stimulate man to do his best. How they thank you with a look! how they rejoice with you! how they comfort you! how often they outdo expectation! and how pretty they are! If they fight against you, what winsome, if not winning, adversaries!'*

Women's clothing was not very helpful in combating these unfortunate stereotypes. In the late 1870s and early 1880s, for example, women simply wore their ordinary day dresses to play lawn tennis. Sleeves were long and skirts often brushed the ground. Wide-brimmed hats made it impossible to see overhead and heeled boots further impaired a lady's movements. Add to that, women playing lawn tennis were expected to wear all the layers of normal dress, including corsets, petticoats, and bustles.

The Orleans tennis apron (left). (*Townsend's Monthly* Selection of Parisian Costumes, 1878)

VICTORIAN SPORTSWEAR

Most ladies of this time period would wear a pinafore or an apron over their day dress to protect it from dirt and grass stains during play. Tennis aprons generally had pockets to store extra tennis balls and were sometimes equipped with a hook on one side on which a lady could hang her racket. They were often made of sturdy fabrics such as twill; however, many fashion magazines of the day describe luxurious tennis aprons made of heavily trimmed silk. For example, the 1880 edition of *Townsend's Monthly Magazine* features the 'Orleans Lawn Tennis Apron,' which is described as being a 'very becoming and ladylike' style, with an 'underskirt of mauve silk' and an apron of 'mauve-flowered satinette' edged in lace.

According to Cunnington, it was not until 1884 that sports costumes for tennis, as well as for archery, boating, shooting, fishing, and cycling, began to form 'a distinct class' in women's fashion. Magazines of the late 1880s advertised stylish tennis dresses made of wool, silk, sateen, or striped flannel with straight or pleated skirts and hems which were often as much as four inches off the ground. As an example, the 1889 edition of the *Woman's World Magazine* includes an illustration of a very fashionable tennis dress by Messrs. Debenham and Freebody. The description reads:

'The model has a skirt of check woollen, blue on white, the bodice made simply to the figure, the novelty about it being some lacings introduced on the collarbone in front, and triple lacings at the waist; the jacket is of plain flannel in pure white, and can be slipped on and off as required. This is just the sort of dress that a true tennis-player would appreciate; it looks well, and insures perfect freedom.'

By the 1890s, women's fashions for lawn tennis were beginning to adapt to the sport. In an article in the *Official Lawn Tennis Bulletin* of 1897, Juliette Atkinson addresses these changes, writing:

'Some years ago it was thought that almost anything would do for a tennis costume; and the result was sometimes appalling. The player of today has rather more idea of the fitness of things, and does not appear on the courts in a woollen skirt, too long and much too heavy, a waist that certainly was never intended for

TENNIS-DRESS.

In the beginning, tennis dresses were no different from ordinary day dresses. (*The Woman's World*, 1889)

the tennis court, and an absurd little visored cap that neither shelters from the sun nor adds to the appearance.'

Atkinson goes on to recommend a plain tennis dress with a full skirt, approximately 'three yards and a half round' and 'made to clear the ground by about four inches'. For fabric, she suggests a lightweight piqué, well starched. As for colour and trimmings, she advises that 'white is prettier for tennis than anything else' and that:

'All ribbons, bows, in fact all fussiness should be dispensed with in the tennis costume. The simpler it is, the better.'

Though women's tennis costumes were much more practical at the end of the Victorian era than they had been in the 1870s, they were still relatively restrictive – especially when compared with tennis costumes of today. Nevertheless, many talented sportswomen of the Victorian era were able to make a name for themselves in competitive play. In 1884, Maud Watson became the first female champion at Wimbledon. She was soon followed by Wimbledon champions Blanche Bingley, Lottie Dodd, Lena Rice, and Charlotte Cooper. Cooper would go on to win the tennis singles event at the Summer Olympics in 1900, making her the first individual female Olympic champion in history.

Golf

Though golf had been played since the fifteenth century, it was not until the Victorian era that it first emerged as a wildly popular sport. Victorian women weren't entirely excluded from the game. In fact, the first women's golf club was founded in 1867 at St. Andrews in Scotland. Unfortunately, the course itself was, as one writer describes it, 'little more than a glorified putting green'.[45] Many gentlemen of the era were perplexed as to why women golfers would require anything more competitive. After all, as an article in the 1889 edition of the *Scots Observer* states:

'Women, of course, can never be as good golfers as men. But this is only because they are not so good at anything they try as men are – not even at packing a bag or flavouring a sauce. Also, it must be allowed, they can never get as much pure amusement from this or from any game.'

Despite the negative stereotypes associated with their sex, lady golfers continued to play – and to compete. An 1896 edition of the *Cosmopolitan* reports on a golf tournament that year in Hoylake where 'lady golfers from all parts of England, Scotland, and Ireland' converged to participate. So popular was the game of golf with the fairer sex that even 'a few white-haired matrons' were counted among the competitors. According to the *Cosmopolitan*:

'It is hard to tell what outdoor pastime rivals this one, among the many other games and exercises that are now in vogue with women as well as men.'

Women's clothing gradually adapted to golfing in much the same way it had adapted to tennis. By the end of the century, ladies were wearing golfing suits made of tweed or waterproof serge in shades of navy blue, grey, or fawn. A golfing suit or golf costume often comprised a belted Norfolk bodice and plain, ankle-length skirt. The 1894 edition of *Cassells Family Magazine* describes the Norfolk bodice as having 'moderately full sleeves' and a 'belt and pockets outlined by leather.' The skirts of golfing suits were also frequently 'outlined at the hem with leather' in order to protect the edge of the skirt from the 'disfiguring' effects of wet grass.

Circular golfing capes were also quite popular with sporting ladies of the late Victorian era, as were speciality golfing skirts. The 1900 edition of *Golf Illustrated* reports that a 'leading tailor' had come up with a speciality skirt that could be worn for either golfing or shooting. It was 'furnished with a small strap or buckle at intervals round the skirt' which allowed for the skirts to be looped up whenever a lady was engaged in sports. When drawn up, it formed 'a sort of folded tunic at the knees' with 'the bottom of the skirt coming to the top of the boots.' When a lady quit the game and returned to the house, her skirt could be let down, after which it is reported to have looked just the same as any other non-sporting skirt.

Ladies of the late Victorian era accessorized their golfing suits with round straw hats with turned up brims that were often trimmed, very simply, with black ribbon. For footwear, they donned dark leather boots or shoes with sensible stockings. Gloves were also required.

Cycling

Though bicycles had been around in some form or another since the mid-nineteenth century, the cycling craze did not truly hit Victorian England until the 1880s. It was then that the safety bicycle was invented. Made with two wheels of identical size, the safety bicycle had pneumatic tires, a chain-driven rear wheel, and what is known as a diamond frame. Safety bicycles were much easier to manage than the heavy bicycles of the past and, as the century came to a close, more and more people were taking up cycling as both a hobby and as a means of transportation

Women were just as keen on cycling as their male counterparts; however, their clothing was often an obstacle. Long, heavy skirts could get tangled in the wheels or the bicycle chain, leading some to advocate for the creation of a new bicycle costume for women comprised of shirtwaists and Bloomer-like trousers. According to the 1895 edition of *Good Health*:

'The most popular bicycle costumes do not include even the slight suggestion of a skirt, and represent the trouser idea in its very highest development.'

Due in large part to the bicycle, Victorian society became much more tolerant of trousers on women than it ever had in the age of the Bloomer costume. As *Good Health* states:

> *'The bicycle seems to have collided with the conventional ideas of dress with so much momentum as to have smashed them, so to speak into "smithereens," and now that the ice is broken, it may be that women will awaken to the fact that conventionalism is not necessary for existence; that a woman can be comfortable and still hold her head as high as any other woman, and be as much respected, and no more gaped at as she walks the streets.'*

Others were not so accepting of the influence of the bicycle on women's clothing. Indeed, to some men, women's athletics as a whole seemed to be a contradiction of their essential femininity. Even doctors who specialized in women's health were not entirely convinced that women's sports and sportswear should be acceptable. For instance, addressing women and the Victorian bicycle craze, an 1896 edition of the *American Journal of Obstetrics and Diseases of Women and Children* relates the opinions of Dr William P. Care, stating:

> *'With the so-called new woman he did not sympathize, but a woman might have a bicycle costume as well as a bathing suit, riding habit, or ballroom dress. But he could not tolerate the "horsey airs" assumed by some of them. It should be understood that there is a great difference between men and women naturally...If a woman undertook to imitate the ways of man she lost her chief attraction.'*

Despite the ambivalence expressed by some members of Victorian society, ladies embraced the bicycle craze wholeheartedly. Long skirts, tight corsets, and high-heeled boots were discarded in exchange for shirtwaists, knickerbockers, and gaiters. Comfort and freedom of movement were paramount. Some women even joined the ranks of Victorian 'scorchers' – those bicyclists with a passion for excessively high, and often dangerous, speeds.

For the average lady bicyclist, cycling publications of the day recommended that, at minimum, she outfit herself with 'knickerbockers, shirtwaist, stockings, shoes, gaiters, sweater, coat...hat and gloves'.[46] Knickerbockers were loose-fitting knee length breeches which buttoned at the waist and at the knee. By the late 1890s, they were widely worn by fashionable lady cyclists in London, Paris, and New York. They were not the most flattering article of clothing – at least as far as men were concerned. When the English theatre critic Clement William Scott encountered a profusion of knickerbocker-wearing lady cyclists in Paris one season, he even went so far as to write:

'If Miss Parisian Knickerbocker only knew how unseemly she looks, she would burn her bike and revert to lace petticoats, for which she was once distinguished.'

Not all lady cyclists were as keen on the fashion for knickerbockers as others. In fact, many felt that knickerbockers were immodest and instead outfitted themselves in cycling costumes comprised of belted jackets and divided skirts. The 1898 edition of the *Delineator* describes one fashionable style of divided skirt that season, writing:

> *'The divided skirt is planned to be exceedingly graceful whether the wearer is mounted or dismounted. Each portion is of circular shaping, with a seam at the inside of the leg, and is fitted over the hip by three darts and ripples prettily below.'*

A lady's cycling costumed with a belted jacket and a divided skirt. (The *Delineator*, 1898)

Some varieties of divided skirts came equipped with straps which could be buttoned onto each side of the skirt in order to 'prevent the skirt from being blown about while riding.'[47] Other cycling costumes featured regular gored skirts with darts at each side which eliminated any unnecessary fullness, allowing the skirts to fit smoothly down over the hips. Cycling skirts came in varying lengths and, along with other cycling costumes, could be found in a range of fabrics, including cotton, linen, tweed, and wool.

Chapter 11

Proper Dress for Marriage, Maternity, and Mourning

'First in the thoughts of the bride-elect stands her wedding gown, about which clings a halo of romance that not all the sorrows of a lifetime can ever quite dispel.'

Godey's Lady's Book, 1894.

Nowhere was fashion more strictly prescribed than in the realm of clothing for marriage, maternity, and mourning. Ladies' magazines, medical journals, and etiquette manuals all offered advice on proper attire for a lady's wedding day, as well as for what she should wear during the course of her pregnancy and for the period in which she mourned the death of a spouse, a parent, or a child. Not every woman adhered to this advice, but for those ladies who wished to remain *à la mode* – and to retain the good opinion of their peers – proper attire during each of these three important stages of a lady's life was of critical concern.

Marriage

For much of the early nineteenth century, bridal fashion as we know it today did not exist. On their wedding day, ladies simply wore their best dresses, whether those dresses be grey, blue, brown, or drab. This practice did not truly begin to change until the 1840 wedding of Queen Victoria to Prince Albert. Theirs was widely acknowledged to be a love match and fascinated royal watchers throughout Europe and America pored over the detailed newspaper and magazine accounts of the grand ceremony at St. James's Palace and the equally grand wedding ensemble worn by the queen.

For her wedding dress, Queen Victoria chose a bridal gown made of 'rich white satin, trimmed with orange blossoms' paired with a wreath of orange blossoms on her head and 'a beautiful veil of Honiton lace'.[48] As the 1840 issue of *Godey's Lady's Book* reports:

'The lace which formed the flounce of the dress, measures four yards, and is three quarters of a yard in depth. The pattern is a rich, and exquisitely

tasteful design, drawn expressly for the purpose, and surpasses any thing that has ever been executed either in England or in Brussels. So anxious was the manufacturer that her Majesty should have a dress perfectly unique, that she has since the completion of the lace destroyed all the designs. The veil, which is of the same material, and was made to correspond, afforded employment to the poor lace workers for more than six weeks. It is a yard and a half square.'

The queen's decision to wear a white wedding dress had far-reaching effects. Soon, fashionable brides were all donning white dresses for their weddings. Not only did white come to represent the purity and chastity of the bride, it also symbolized the affluence of her family. Unlike dresses made in shades of blue, brown, or other colours, white could not be easily laundered and re-worn on subsequent occasions. This made it an expensive choice, reserved for those in society who could afford the extravagance of a dress that would be worn once and—very likely—never worn again.

As the century progressed, whites and creams continued to be the most popular shades for wedding dresses, as well as the most costly. Brides were encouraged to

Queen Victoria is credited with making white wedding dresses fashionable. (*Magasin Des Demoiselles*, March 1849. Thomas J. Watson Library, Metropolitan Museum of Art)

use an excess of fabric, even when their gown was of the simple variety. According to the 1885 edition of *Household Words*:

> *'Nothing spoils a bridal-dress like any appearance of skimpiness. The train should be long, the draperies ample; and this is no more difficult in a plain material than in a costly one.'*

Wedding dresses came in a variety of fabrics. In addition to white or cream satin there were bridal gowns made in cotton, muslin, organdie, and silk. There were also lavish bridal gowns made with 'the costliest lace,' panels of 'broché velvet' or 'silver brocade,' and petticoats embroidered with pearls.[49] Bridal veils were often made of lace and fastened back from the face with jewelled pins. As to the bride's shoes, they mirrored the fashionable style of the decade – whether boots, pumps, or slippers – and were generally made in white satin or kid.

Brides accessorized their wedding ensembles with either real or wax flowers. Orange blossoms remained a perennial favourite throughout the Victorian era, but roses, lilies, and lilacs were also quite popular. Flowers could be worn in the hair, used to trim the bridal hat, or worked into the design of the gown itself. In addition, most brides carried a bouquet of flowers. As the 1899 edition of the *Delineator* reports:

Victorian brides were encouraged not to skimp on their fabric and trimmings. (*La Mode Illustree*, 1879. Thomas J. Watson Library, Metropolitan Museum of Art)

'The bride this season usually carries a shower bouquet of some favorite white flowers; or, if she prefers, a silk or satin-covered prayer-book tipped with gold is selected.'

Maternity

When it came to clothing, Victorian maternity manuals advised that the expectant mother let comfort be her guide. However, as a rule, tight corsets were discouraged, as were any form-fitting garments which might impede either the pregnant woman's circulation or the growth of the foetus. In fact, as Dr John West explains in his 1887 book *Maidenhood and Motherhood*:

'The French term enceinte *was originally applied to pregnant women from a habit of laying aside the belt or girdle which they were otherwise accustomed to wear; hence, the term enceinte means to be unbound, and has come to be applied to women in ante-confinement motherhood.'*

Not only were tight clothes a danger to a lady's health, they were also seen as not particularly modest for a woman in the more visible stages of pregnancy. According to West:

'While there is no demand that the mother make an undue advertisement of her state, which would be as immodest as the attempts at its concealment, it is eminently desirable that her dress, especially about those parts of her body which are the regions of procreative life, be worn quite loosely.'

Some Victorian maternity dresses adjusted to fit the figure. The 1890 edition of *Good Health* describes one such variety which featured 'lacings in the dart seams and transverse lacings at the waist line'. The lacings were hidden by draped fabric at the front of the dress, allowing the dress to be let out as a woman's pregnancy progressed. The designer of the dress is reported as stating that 'motherhood is robbed of half its dignity by the way in which most expectant mothers dress'. She advised that rather than 'fixing up old dresses no matter how ugly and worn,' pregnant ladies should instead 'take special care to robe themselves neatly and gracefully'.

Mourning

The Victorians had strict rules of mourning which outlined where a lady was allowed to go and what she was allowed to wear. Much of this depended on the relation of the deceased to the woman in question. Husbands merited the deepest period of mourning, with strict etiquette demanding that a lady mourn her departed spouse for two years. Deceased parents or children were generally mourned for one year, while deceased grandparents or siblings merited a mourning period of only six months.

Just as with wedding dresses, the style for fashionable mourning was set by Queen Victoria herself. When her husband, Prince Albert, died in 1861, the queen went into deep mourning for the remainder of her life. She favoured unrelieved black crepe, leading an 1895 edition of the *Delineator* to state that:

> '*The Royal Widow of England has fixed the fashions for all the widows of her realm and of America. The orthodox livery of widow's woe is "an experiment in the utmost laying on of crape."*'

In addition to black crepe, ladies in deep mourning were permitted to wear 'serges, bombazines, delaine, barège, and merino,' fabrics which were all considered to be 'suitable materials for the deepest mourning'.[50] Black mourning dress could be accented with a black cashmere shawl, a veiled bonnet of plain, black crepe, and black kid gloves. Some authorities advised that no jewellery or ornamentation of any kind was permitted except jet and only then in the form of buttons or clasps used to fasten the collar, cuffs, and belt. Others allowed women in deep mourning to continue to wear their pearls and 'plainly-set solitaire diamonds,' but prohibited any coloured stones, such as sapphires, rubies, or emeralds.[51]

Ladies in light mourning were permitted to wear dresses in black and white, grey, mauve, violet, or some combination thereof. Dresses of solid mauve or violet were considered appropriate for light mourning. In fact, many widows in the final months of their second year of mourning exchanged their heavy black crepe for a subdued silk dress in some variety of purple. This could be accented with lace or embroidery at the collar and cuffs, jet jewellery set in gold, and a bonnet trimmed with ribbons and even a few crepe flowers.

Ladies in deep mourning wore black from head to toe. (*Freja: Illustrerad Skandinavisk Modetidning*, 1885. Nordic Museum, Sweden)

PART III

Beauty

Chapter 12

Victorian Hair Care

'All writers, sacred and profane, ancient and modern, join in praising with unstinted terms the advantages which personal comeliness derives from a handsome head of hair.'
Personal Beauty by D. G. Brinton, M.D., 1870.

Since biblical times, a woman's hair has been known as her crowning glory. This was never more true than in the Victorian era, a span of years during which thick, glossy hair was one of the primary measures of a lady's beauty. To care for her hair, a Victorian lady employed a range of products and techniques. Some of these were fairly simple and common-sense strategies to cleanse or de-tangle her tresses. Others were more extreme methods designed to stimulate growth, change the colour, or cure unfortunate maladies such as a dandruff or an oily scalp.

Brushing, Combing, and Cleansing

One of the most important components of a Victorian lady's hair care routine was cleansing the hair of oil and dirt. Unfortunately, shampoo as we know it today did not exist during the nineteenth century. In fact, the word shampoo meant something quite different to the Victorians. Derived from the Hindi word *champo*, it was an Indian technique of pressing or massaging the scalp and other parts of the body. In her 1840 book *Female Beauty, as Preserved and Improved by Regimen, Cleanliness and Dress*, Mrs Walker describes the Indian practice of shampooing as follows:

'One of the servants of the bath stretches you on a plank, and sprinkles you with warm water. He next presses the whole body with the palms of his hands, and cracks the joints of the fingers, legs, arms, and other members. He then turns you over on your stomach; kneels upon the loins; and taking hold of the shoulders, makes the spine crack by acting upon all the vertebrae, and strikes some sharp blows upon the most fleshy and muscular parts, &c.'

As evidenced by the above description, Victorian shampooing was not the ideal method to cleanse one's hair of everyday dirt and grime. In order to do that, most ladies had a complete regimen of haircare which encompassed everything from regimented brushing to egg washes and perfumed pomades made of bear grease. To begin, Victorian ladies were advised to possess themselves – at the minimum – of at least three combs made of tortoiseshell with blunt teeth of varying widths; a 'hard or penetrating brush' to clean the roots of the hair after combing; and a brush made of 'very fine hairs' or 'fine rice roots' which was used to smooth the hair.[52] Regular use of the brush for ten minutes twice a day, morning and evening, was believed to clear the hair and scalp of 'scurf and dust' and to 'preserve its bright and glossy appearance.'[53]

Advice on hair brushing did not change much throughout the Victorian era. Indeed, by the end of the century, the amount of time that most ladies' magazines

A woman seated at her dressing table having her hair brushed by her maid. (Wellcome Library, London. Creative Commons Attribution 4.0 International Public License)

Oh who would be a lady's maid,
And toil from morn till night,
By artificial means to make
A beauty from a fright
My misstress is so trying,
Her clothes are grand and fine,
My only consolation is,
I know they'll soon be mine.

and beauty manuals advised that a lady should spend brushing her hair had actually increased. For example, an 1889 issue of *Good Housekeeping* directs its readers to:

> *'Brush the head twice each day with a bristle-brush, not too stiff, but sufficiently so to penetrate the scalp. Brush "every which way," – forward, backward, up, down and sideways. This process will invigorate and soften the hair. Fifteen minutes twice a day devote to it if you have the time.'*

Added to this twice-daily ritual of brushing and combing, Mrs Walker states that, if needed, 'ablutions with lukewarm water, or soap and water' may also be employed to keep one's tresses in tiptop shape. In most circumstances, this was all that was required. However, on occasion the Victorian lady might need to give her hair a really thorough wash. This was often easier said than done. Washing the hair was an arduous undertaking – a task which some women would much rather avoid, even if it meant having hair that was less than clean. As *Sylvia's Book of the Toilet* (1881) explains:

> *'Many women who are models of cleanliness in other respects are careless about the hair, partly because washing it "is such a business," and partly from the mistaken but rather general idea that frequent washing injures the chevelure.'*

In order to wash her hair, a lady first had to wet it thoroughly. During much of the Victorian era, this was done by means of a washbasin and pitcher. Later, piped in water would make the task a little less inconvenient. Once her hair was wet, a lady could apply a cleanser of her choosing. Many beauty manuals of the nineteenth century suggested a mixture made of eggs beaten to a cream. In the early part of the era, Mrs Walker recommended:

> *'The yolks of a couple of eggs, beat till they form a cream, to be rubbed into the hair, and then washed out with tepid water, well brushed and wiped, as bestowing the most silky and beautiful appearance.'*

While the 1892 book *Beauty, It's Attainment and Preservation* advised ladies with dry hair to use only the yolks of the eggs, stating:

> *'When the roots of the hair and the scalp have been thoroughly impregnated with the egg, they and the hair may be washed with warm water and pure Castile or some other equally fine soap, after which a copious rinsing should follow.'*

Although favoured by many fine ladies – including Empress Elisabeth of Austria who is known to have washed her hair with a mixture of raw eggs and fine cognac – egg washes were not the only option for thoroughly cleansing one's hair. In *Beeton's Book of Household Management* (1861), Isabella Beeton offers a recipe for 'A Good Wash for the Hair' made of a combination of 'one pennyworth' of borax, a half pint of olive oil, and one pint of boiling water, while Mrs Walker provides detailed instructions on washing long tresses with a combination of warm water and perfumed toilet soap, writing:

> *'A basin of warm water, rendered frothy with a little toilet soap slightly perfumed, will answer the purpose. It is necessary to remove carefully the tresses of the hair, and with a sponge, dipped in the soapy water, to wash it thoroughly all over. The hair being perfectly cleansed, the head should be well dried with napkins, slightly warmed in winter, and then brushed several times.'*

Nowadays washing one's hair every day or every other day is often the norm for most people. For the Victorian lady, the frequency of a thorough wash with egg yolks or perfumed soap and water was wholly dependent on the nature of her hair. If her hair was oily, she was advised to wash it every eight days. By contrast, fine hair on which a lady rarely used pomades or other products could go much longer between washings. If the hair was too fine to tolerate washing on a regular basis, the 1885 *Art of Living* advises its readers to utilize a concoction comprised of:

> *'Three pennyworth each of castor oil and spirits of rosemary; a wineglassful of Jamaica rum; and half a pint of clean rain water.'*

These ingredients were then put into a bottle and shaken up before being applied to the roots of the hair with a sponge or a flannel. The *Art of Living* claims that if a lady applied 'a tablespoon twice a day' and then brushed it out until her hair was 'quite dry,' this concoction never failed to immediately 'thicken and beauty' fine hair, as well as to prevent it from falling out.

There were also alternatives to washing for oily hair. Before retiring to bed in the evening, a lady might use a Swan's-down puff to apply a light dusting of rice meal, orrisroot, or Florence iris powder to her scalp and tresses. The powder would act as an absorbent during the night and, in the morning, could be brushed out.

In most cases regular washing and brushing were enough to ensure the health and cleanliness of a lady's hair. However, those ladies suffering from dandruff were obliged to employ additional measures. For mild to moderate dandruff, *Good Housekeeping* prescribes a wash comprised of 'two ounces pulverized borax' and 'two ounces of gum camphor' boiled together in one quart of water. The contents were then strained, diluted, and applied to the head with a cloth made of flannel. For severe dandruff, medical journals recommended 'dilute acids' or 'aromatic substances and balsams, such as benzoin and Peru balsam.'[54]

Hair Oils, Potions, and Pomades

Based on the above descriptions of hair brushing and washing, it may seem as though there was nothing overly extravagant about haircare in the Victorian era. However, crimping, curling, elaborate pinning, tight plaiting, and other fashionable nineteenth century means of styling one's hair did take a toll. As a result, ladies were compelled to turn to all sorts of oils, potions, and pomades to restore lustre to their brittle and fading locks.

One of the most popular treatments of the era was Rowland's Macassar Oil. Advertised as a 'delightfully fragrant and transparent preparation for the hair' and as an 'invigorator and beautifier beyond all precedent,' Macassar oil was applied to the tresses by both men and women to restore gloss and sheen. As with any preparation of this sort, it did have some visible effect, but the primary result of using Macassar oil was not the one the inventors intended. In her 2009 book *Compacts and Cosmetics*, Madeleine Marsh explains:

> '*What it certainly did leave was greasy marks on the furniture—hence the introduction of the antimacassar (a little cloth designed to protect the chair back).*'

Rowland's Macassar Oil was not the only nineteenth century hair treatment. There was Ayer's Hair Vigor, Edwards' Harlene for the Hair, and Hall's Vegetable Sicilian Hair Renewer, to name just a few. These products promised everything, up to and including curing baldness and 'restoring grey hair to its original colour.' Mrs Walker was sceptical of these claims, wisely advising her readers:

> '*The hair sometimes turns partially grey before that age at which such a change may naturally be expected. This is a calamity particularly disagreeable to females, because it makes them appear older than they really are; but no one, save quacks, impostors and charlatans, professes to have found any means of obviating it.*'

This did not mean that Victorian ladies had no way of masking greyness. There were hair dyes even then, though dying one's hair was still not considered to be wholly respectable. Some critics of the era even went so far as to give the act of dying one's hair a moral dimension, claiming that 'to dye the hair is to practise an intentional deception'.[55] These pronouncements had little effect on those women who were desperate to cover up their grey, or to change their dark hair to a fashionable shade of gold or auburn. In order to do so, many ladies applied potentially harmful potions containing nitrate of silver, sulphate of copper, potash, or lead. Less harmful were hair lighteners made with infusions of saffron mixed with carbonate of soda. These were often followed by applications of lemon juice and vinegar which promised to give 'a reddish yellow hue to dark-coloured hair'.[56]

An 1890s
advertisement for
Edwards' Harlene
for the Hair.
(Wellcome Library,
London. Creative
Commons Attribution
4.0 International
Public License)

As an aid to styling, pomade was often used. It was especially recommended for smoothing down plaits and for imparting a shine to both real hair and to the fake 'tufts' which were frequently incorporated into Victorian hairstyles to add fullness. Pomade was also used as a treatment to alleviate the extreme dryness which resulted from curling and crimping hair with hot irons.

A variety of pomade made with perfumed bear grease was popular until the final quarter of the century when, as Marsh reports, 'vegetal lotions—made from coconut, palm and olive oils—had largely taken over'. Until that time, there were a few other ways of making pomade that, thankfully, did not require the boiled fat of a Russian brown bear. Isabella Beeton provides several recipes for pomade in her book of household management, including one which contains nothing more than lard, castor oil, and scent.

With hair washed, brushed, oiled, and pomaded, all that was left was for a lady to arrange her hair into one of the many intricate Victorian hairstyles of the day.

Chapter 13

Victorian Hairstyles and Hairdressing

'A lady may modify, twist, invert, and crisp, coil, plait, and do what she pleases; but after all it must be acknowledged that there is nothing (in hair-dressing, at least) new under the sun.'

The *Art of Beauty* by Madame Bayard, 1876.

In the Victorian era, it was not enough to have clean, healthy, lustrous tresses. Those tresses must be twisted, rolled, plaited, and pinned into suitably fashionable styles. Dressing the hair in this manner was practically an art form and, as the styles were always evolving, it required a lady – or a lady's maid – to pay constant attention to changing trends in fashionable coiffures, as illustrated and explained in any one of the numerous nineteenth century lady's magazines and beauty books.

Hairstyling Basics

In order to style her hair, a lady needed to use more than a simple brush and comb. Beauty manuals of the day recommended that she possess a range of tools, including curling tongs, a selection of hair combs, pins, pomade, and a supply of false hair. False hair came in a variety of forms, including invisible tufts, comb tufts, plaits, ringlets, and pads. Used to add height, thickness, or simply as fashionable adornment, false hair was meant to blend seamlessly with one's own hair colour. For an exact match, many women made their own hairpieces—called 'rats'—out of the excess hair which accumulated in their hair brushes and combs.[57]

To curl their hair, Victorian women employed curling tongs. These were heated directly in the fire and, as a result, it was difficult to control the temperature. Hair was frequently scorched or burned off completely. According to *Sylvia's Book of the Toilet*, the safest method for using curling tongs was to:

'Fold the hair, having slightly damped it, over the frizzing or curling tongs, having previously carefully wrapped these round with a roll of thin brown paper. Or, do the hair upon stout crimping pins, or braid it in and out of a loop of thick cord; fold a piece of thin paper over the crimp, and the pinching iron may be used in safety.'

Though new hair products were always on the market, the basic hairdressing items listed above did not change much throughout the Victorian era. Equipped with brush, combs, curling tongs, false hair, pins, and pomade and armed with a variety of trimmings such as beads, ribbons, feathers, and fresh flowers, a lady could create almost any style from 1837 through 1901.

Hairstyles of the 1840s

During the late 1830s and into the 1840s, hairstyles were very much in keeping with the stark, Gothic gowns that were fashionable at the beginning of the Victorian era. Hair was generally worn close to the head and smoothed down to completely cover the ears. Most styles were parted in the centre, pinned up or braided at the back, and then coiled or curled into clusters of ringlets on each side of the face. Hair could also be arranged in smooth bands which swept down over the ears before being drawn back into a simple plait or chignon at the nape of the neck.

The 1837 edition of the *Lady's Magazine* features a plate depicting three popular styles that year. They are described as being 'precisely the same' with minor differences. As the *Lady's Magazine* states:

> *'The style of coiffure of the first three heads is … ornamented with a bandeau of pearls – the second which gives the coiffure in front with flowers, and the third likewise with flowers, giving the back of the other two. The hair for this coiffure is brought in smooth bands, as low as possible, at the sides of the face, where after forming a kind of chignon at each side, it is turned up again (see plate); the back hair is tied very low, and formed into a single coque or bow, surrounded by braids and circles of hair, an ornamented arrow runs through the whole; three full blown white roses are placed at each side of the face.'*

Three fashionable, early Victorian hairstyles. (*The Lady's Magazine*, 1837)

A centre part hairstyle with ringlets is depicted in this fashion plate from 1844. (Thomas J. Watson Library, Metropolitan Museum of Art)

By 1840, *Godey's Lady's Book* reports that ladies were dressing the front of their hair in 'long ringlets in very full tufts, plain bands, or bands with the ends braided and turned up again.' The back of their hair was generally worn low on the neck, either coiled in braids or braided in the form of a figure eight. For evening, fashionable hairstyles were often ornamented with flowers or jewellery. For example, the 1841 issue of the *New Monthly Belle Assemblée* features a Paris evening dress paired with a hairstyle described as being:

> *'Disposed in ringlets on each side, and a low knot behind; the ringlets are looped back on each side by roses; a fancy jewellery bandeau, and a bird of Paradise; the latter placed quite at the back of head, complete the coiffure.'*

Even young Queen Victoria was known to wear her hair with a simple centre parting and the sides smoothed down over her ears and braided low or looped on each side.

Hairstyles of the 1850s

By the 1850s, women's hairstyles were becoming slightly less severe. Though hair was still parted in the centre, it was now worn puffed at the sides and was often styled with heavy ringlets or 'drooping clusters of curls' at the temples.[58] The back

Two ladies with their hair arranged in the popular rolled bandeau style. (Detail from *Les Modes Parisiennes*, 1856. Thomas J. Watson Library, Metropolitan Museum of Art)

of the hair was generally drawn into a small to moderately-sized bun and pinned at the nape of the neck.

One of the most fashionable hairstyles of the 1850s was the rolled bandeau style or 'bandeau bouffant.' It was created with the aid of the 'Mainnier bandeau,' a hair band worn in conjunction with a tightly braided lock of hair at the front that was fixed in place by a comb. This served as a foundation over which the rest of the hair was arranged. A version of this called the 'coiffure Eugénie' was particularly popular during the 1850s. Inspired by a style worn by the Empress Eugénie herself, the Mainnier bandeau was divided into two equal parts, 'reserving in the middle a small lock that was tightly plaited' and 'fixed by a comb'.[59] According to author August Challamel's 1882 book, *The History of Fashion in France*:

> '*With the help of the Mainnier bands, the Eugénie coiffure formed a roll that increased in size from above the forehead until it reached the ear, where one or two curls falling on the neck completed the arrangement.*'

The rolled bandeau style could be modified according to one's taste. Fashion magazines offered many different takes on the popular coiffure. For example, the 1856 edition of the *Ladies' Companion and Monthly Magazine* contains a fashion plate which depicts ladies wearing their hair in various versions of the rolled bandeau style. One lady is described as having hair that is 'well crisped at the top, so as to form a bandeau bouffant, which is prolonged very low on the neck like a large full curl turned under.'

The rolled bandeau hairstyle is shown, both plain and accented with heavy braids. (Detail from *Les Modes Parisiennes Reunies*, 1856. Thomas J. Watson Library, Metropolitan Museum of Art)

More elaborate still is the bandeau coiffure described in an 1856 issue of *Mrs Stephens' Illustrated New Monthly*, in which the back of the lady's hair was 'arranged in four smooth flat loops, arranged in the form of a bow, and encircled by a wide Grecian braid'. This intricate pattern was complemented by flat loops of braid on either side of the head and a rolled bandeau at the front which was 'surmounted by a *couronne* of Grecian braids'.

Ladies of the 1850s accessorized their hair with ribbons, flowers, seed pearls, and ostrich plumes. Some bound their hair into hair nets made of silk or of 'gold and silver twist' ornamented with bugles and beads.[60] Hair nets were especially fashionable with evening dress and ball gowns.

Hairstyles of the 1860s

By the 1860s, women's hairstyles were becoming much fuller and more feminine. Hair was now plaited, twisted into large rolls, or swept back into a chignon or a hairnet. Quite a few of the popular hairstyles featured plaits combined with rolls. These were twisted and woven together into patterns. Though women's magazines of the day recommended certain ways of doing this, there was no hard and fast rule about the exact placement of the plaits. The rolls, however, were usually situated at the nape of the neck or at the sides of the face.

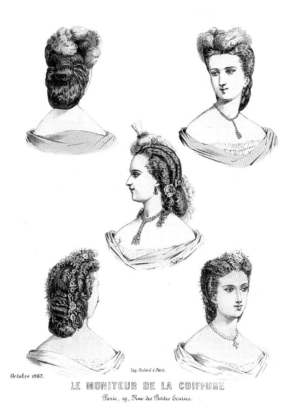

A selection of fashionable hairstyles from the 1860s. (*Le Moniteur de la Coiffure*, October 1863. Thomas J. Watson Library, Metropolitan Museum of Art)

Often, the roll was built up in size over a pad of false hair and secured with a thick plait. This plait was frequently made of false hair as well. Alternatively, the roll itself could be made of false hair secured with a lady's own hair plaited around it.

Though rolls and plaits were suitable for day-to-day wear, formal occasions often required something more elaborate. Many ladies crimped and rolled their hair off their face and back over a cushion. At the nape of the neck, the hair was then arranged into the shape of a bow. This was a very popular style for eveningwear in the mid-1860s. As the 1863 edition of *Godey's Lady's Book* explains:

> *'The bow at the back can be arranged with the natural hair, or it can be made of a false braid. In the latter case, it is pinned on underneath the back hair, which should be tied and combed over the bow, twisted round and fastened with a fancy comb.'*

Bow coiffures could be extraordinarily elaborate and were often accented with beads, jewels, combs, or gold and silver hair ornaments.

LE MONITEUR DE LA COIFFURE
Paris, 19, Rue des Petites Écuries.

For evening, some ladies arranged their hair into the form of a bow or adorned their coiffure with flowers. (Le Moniteur de la Coiffure, October 1863. Thomas J. Watson Library, Metropolitan Museum of Art)

For balls and eveningwear, many ladies chose to adorn their hair with wreaths of flowers such as orange blossoms, rosebuds, or verbena. Flowers could also be attached to a decorated bandeau or hair ribbon. Most commonly of all, flowers were simply pinned into the rolls or plaits of an evening coiffure. For a more intricate style, some 1860s coiffures featured multiple layers of rolls, each one trimmed with flowers between.

Many ladies of the 1860s bound their tresses up in nets. The styles of these hair nets varied widely. There was the popularly advertised 'Invisible Hair-Net,' made of fine silk that was virtually indistinguishable from one's natural hair. There were nets made of chenille and those made of gold net, velvet, or narrow strips of leather 'caught together in diamonds by steel, jet, or gilt beads'.[61] Some were suitable for everyday wear, including athletic pursuits such as horseback riding. In fact, according to the 1863 edition of *The Englishwoman's Domestic Magazine*, hair nets were an absolute necessity for ladies venturing out of doors as they kept the hair neat and tidy.

Plain, everyday nets were worn either on their own or accented with 'knots or bows of ribbon over the forehead or at the side of the head.' Other nets were elaborately beaded or adorned with gemstones or feathers, making them suitable for eveningwear.

Hairstyles of the 1870s

Hairstyles in the 1870s were longer and fuller, thus necessitating a greater use of hairpieces and pads. These hairpieces were generally pre-styled into rolls, plaits, or curls so that they could be easily pinned or combed into a lady's existing coiffure where needed. One of the most popular varieties of false hair were the short curls or ringlets that ladies of the 1870s wore over their foreheads. For many ladies who preferred not to cut their hair short in the front, artificial forehead curls were an absolute necessity.

Those ladies who chose not to wear false hair in this manner instead crimped the front of their hair with a hot iron. As another alternative, the 1874 issue of *Godey's Lady's Book* advises that ladies could get the front of their hair to 'wave very nicely' by arranging it into tiny, wet plaits each night before bed. When appropriately crimped or waved, hair at the front of the face was parted in the centre, with the curled hair arranged on either side of the part.

While the front of the hair was styled short, the back of the hair was generally quite long. It was often crimped or arranged in ringlets. The 16 July 1873 edition of the London weekly magazine *Bow Bells* describes three fashionable styles that season,

False hair and accessories.
(*Godey's Lady's Book*, 1873.
Courtesy of Accessible Archives)

Fig. 3.—LADY's COIFFURE. FRONT.—[See Fig. 4.]

Fig. 2.—LADY's COIFFURE.

Fig. 1.—LADY's COIFFURE.

Fig. 4.—LADY's COIFFURE.—BACK. [See Fig. 3.]

A selection of fashionable ladies' coiffures from the early 1870s. (*Harper's Bazaar*, 1873)

including one with the hair 'raised at the back and on the temples' and another with the hair disposed in waves with 'two little curls, detached, upon the forehead' and the hair 'raised from the temples, forming a bandeau or diadem of loops'.

When not worn loose, the back of the hair was often arranged in plaits. The most popular styles of plaits during the 1870s were Grecian plaits, basket plaits, and cable plaits. Nets were another fashionable option for the back of the hair; however, ladies were encouraged not to fall into the 'slovenly habit of just brushing the hair into a tail and then passing a net over it'.[62] This resulted in a net that was only half filled with hair. Instead, they were advised that their hair should first be styled into waves or discreetly supplemented with padding before being gathered up within the confines of the net. As the *Art of Beauty* explains, 'no hair is sufficiently abundant to fill out a net well without some care in arrangement'.

Ladies of the 1870s ornamented their hair with decorative combs made of tortoise-shell or silver or gold. Large, Spanish-style combs were considered to be particularly fashionable. For evening, many adorned their hair with flowers.

Hairstyles of the 1880s

By the 1880s, hairstyles had grown higher at the top and were generally styled shorter at both the back and the front. The back and crown were often twisted, coiled, and plaited. The 1885 issue of the *Domestic Monthly* reports that basket plaits were still very much in style, as was the French twist. At the same time, shorter styles made hairnets obsolete. As the 1883 edition of *Myra's Threepenny Journal* states:

'We fear that nothing can be done to re-introduce the mode of wearing hairnets; with the present style of coiffure they are not in the least needed, and we see no prospect of a change at present.'

Hairstyles of the 1880s often featured short curls, puffs, or a fringe high on the forehead. (Hairstyles, *The Season*, March 1888. Thomas J. Watson Library, Metropolitan Museum of Art)

During the 1880s, the front of the hair was worn loosely waved or arranged into short curls or puffs which covered the upper part of the forehead. These short curls both stood out from and framed the face and, in some cases, extended down to conceal 'the tops of the ears'.[63] In addition to curls and puffs, it was also becoming quite popular to wear a fringe of hair (or bangs) cut across the forehead. *Sylvia's Book of the Toilet* addresses this somewhat controversial trend, stating:

> *'Some persons continue to consider it "fast" to wear a fringe of hair on the forehead. This is a mistake, for it has now become an almost universal custom to wear it, and what is general can never be "fast".'*

False hair and toupees were one option for creating a fashionable 1880s coiffure. (Natural Toupee, *Myra's Threepenny Journal*, 1882)

Fast or no, there were not many women who wished to cut a dramatically short fringe across their forehead; nor very many who wished to go through the trouble of crimping and waving the front of their hair on a daily basis. As a substitute, ladies of the 1880s often employed artificial hair in the form of false fringes, frontelettes, and toupees that had already been curled and frizzed in the prevailing fashion. These could be easily pinned into a lady's natural hair. Some styles, such as the Natural Toupee designed by Mr. Lichtenfeld of Great Portland Street in London, could even be combed and brushed without affecting the arrangement of the artificial hair.

Hairstyles of the 1890s

During the final years of the Victorian era, fashionable coiffures changed with some regularity. Nevertheless, ladies' magazines and beauty books advised their readers not to follow the fashion, but instead to study the shape of their head and face and to choose their coiffure accordingly. This was especially true in relation to the popular style of wearing a short fringe across the forehead. For example, on round faces, a straight fringe was believed to give the face 'a common, vulgar appearance'.[64] Instead, round-faced ladies were counselled to wear their fringe 'slightly pointed at the centre' in order to 'break a set line above the eyebrows"[65]

While the front of the hair was usually styled in short curls or a fringe, the back of the hair could be arranged in a large twist pinned at the neck or in a top knot secured high at the back of the head. Unlike the severe look of the 1840s, these styles were comprised of loose, feminine waves which often appeared to be piled up on top of the head in voluptuous disarray. In America, these styles were typified by the pompadour hairstyle known as the 'Gibson Girl'. Inspired by women depicted in the satirical cartoons of Charles Dana Gibson, the Gibson Girl hairstyle was all the rage during the 1890s and early twentieth century.

In late 1890s England, ladies wore a hairstyle similar to the Gibson Girl. It was called simply the Pompadour coiffure and was created with the aid of a pad of false hair which was made long enough to circle the head. According to one 1898 newspaper report, the hair was first set in waves, after which it was 'parted from the crown to the ears, and then combed loosely back over the pad'.[66] The back of

Hairstyles of the 1890s often featured soft, feminine waves pinned up at the back. (*Standard Designer*, November 1896. Thomas J. Watson Library, Metropolitan Museum of Art)

the hair was then drawn loosely up toward the crown where it was secured with a piece of ribbon. The remaining long strands of hair could be curled or pinned into rolls or tiny puffs.

By the turn of the century, false hair was gradually beginning to fall out of favour. Women were more active and artificial fringe and toupees were no longer practical, particularly for those ladies who cycled or engaged in competitive sports. Nevertheless, the long popularity of the Gibson Girl and Pompadour coiffure – styles which remained in fashion for two decades – necessitated that many ladies continue arranging their locks over a rat or pad of artificial hair in order to achieve a pompadour of sufficient density and height.

For daywear, hair of the 1890s was generally left unadorned. The 25 April 1899 edition of the *Sheffield Evening Telegraph* reports:

> '*Elaborate ornaments are not now being worn in the hair, success depends upon the freshness and glossy appearance of one's tresses and their arrangement so as to suit the features whether viewed profile or full face.*'

By contrast, an evening coiffure was often accented with feathers, decorative combs, or jewelled pins. Some ladies wore flowers pinned into their hair or tucked behind one of their ears. Rosettes made of velvet with rhinestones, diamonds, or other gems at the centre were also quite popular for decorating the coiffure.

Chapter 14

Victorian Skin Care

'The complexion has, probably, more than any other portion or attribute of the human frame, occupied the thoughts of those who devote themselves to the cares of the toilet.'

Sylvia's Book of the Toilet, 1881

In an age when respectable women generally did not wear make-up, the clarity of a lady's complexion was considered to be one of the principal components of her beauty. To that end, Victorian women employed a great many methods to keep their skin soft, smooth, and blemish free, from the most basic soap and water washes to nineteenth century iodine facials, arsenic creams, and patent cosmetics that reached the heights of Victorian quackery.

Health and Lifestyle

Victorians believed that a woman's complexion was a direct result of her lifestyle and her state of mind. Beauty manuals, lady's magazines, and medical journals all emphasized the importance of healthy living and a cheerful attitude. According to an 1849 issue of the *Water Cure Journal*:

'The best way of securing a good complexion is to lay in a stock of good health and good temper, and take care to keep up the supply...We know of no cosmetic equal to the sunny smile. It gives the grace of beauty to the swarthy hue, and makes even freckles and pockmarks passable.'

Victorians also believed that, for women, excess of any kind – whether it be good or bad – was harmful to the skin. As the 1841 *Handbook of the Toilette* explains:

'Goodness of complexion, whether the skin be fair or brown, is incompatible with excess of bodily or mental labour, or excess of pleasure and dissipation.'

This belief that a female's good complexion required little more than a quiet life and a quiet mind coalesced rather conveniently with Victorian values. Unfortunately, the result of this wrong-headed reasoning was that, when a woman presented with a skin condition, it was often believed to be caused by a debauched and dissolute lifestyle. For example, in his 1841 book *A Few Words upon Form and Features*, Arthur Freeling asserts that rosacea is a purely masculine disease, writing:

> 'Ladies seldom suffer from this frightful eruption, as it is usually caused by habits to which ladies are, we hope, never addicted – habitual potations of wine, spirits, beer! Faugh! the very enumeration of such potations in the same page that the sex is mentioned, is almost an insult to it.'

Though the importance of good health and a happy disposition was reiterated constantly, this did not mean that Victorian ladies had no other methods for improving or maintaining their complexions. Women of the Victorian era had rituals and recipes for all of the skin issues we face today.

Cleansing

Victorian women were advised to wash their faces with soap and water using a sponge, washcloth, or soft facial brush. Soap was believed to thoroughly cleanse the skin without irritation. It came in a variety of formulations, including perfumed soaps, medicated soaps, and gentle soaps such as Castile soap and the soap produced by Pears. As for alternative cleansing agents in the form of cosmetic washes and powders, an article in the 1846 issue of the *Eclectic Magazine* states:

> 'Other means than soap for the purification of the skin are highly objectionable, such as the various wash powders: they are sluttish expedients, half doing their work, and leaving all the corners unswept.'

Objections to wash powders persisted throughout the Victorian era. In his 1876 treatise *Healthy Skin*, Sir Erasmus Wilson, a professor of Dermatology at the Royal College of Surgeons, claims that wash powders were incapable of entering the pores of the skin 'otherwise than to obstruct them'. He goes on to assert that ladies who used wash powders instead of soap were recognizable by the tone of their complexions – a tone he likens to a picture 'in which dirt and time have softened and matured the tints'.

These criticisms did not prevent cosmetic washes from being widely used. Some ladies even made their own facial washes at home out of ingredients such as pulverized soap and carbonate of soda. *The Era Formulary* of 1897 contains one such recipe for a powdered cosmetic wash which, when added to water, was purported to not only have 'an agreeable odour,' but also to cleanse and soften the skin.

Victorian medical journals and ladies' magazines advised that soap was the best product for cleansing the face. (Advertisement for Pears Soap, 1886)

Facial waters were another popular, though generally ineffective, method for cleansing the skin. At the beginning of the era, a great many ladies washed their faces with rose water – a product which was used more for its fragrance than for its ability to clean the complexion of dirt and oil. As the 1837 *Book of Health and Beauty* explains:

> *'Though rose water does not possess many virtues as a cosmetic, the ladies use a good deal of it, in consequence of its agreeable smell, and perhaps, also, on account of its name, consecrated to the Loves and the Graces.'*

Ladies also used facial waters or 'cosmetic juice' made with strawberries, lemon, and alcohol.[67] Depending on the recipe, these were purported to do everything from purifying the pores to lightening the complexion.

Moisturizing

Next to soap, cold cream was the most important beauty product in a Victorian lady's arsenal. Sometimes referred to as a 'pomade for the complexion,' cold cream was used to soften and moisturize the skin. It was applied after washing the face. *The Handbook of the Toilette* advises:

> *'Every morning, the face and hands, and that part of the neck of ladies which is exposed to view, as also their arms, may likewise receive a portion of cold cream, to be well rubbed in with a towel.'*

Ingredients in cold cream varied. There were countless recipes available which called for everything from hog's lard and white wax to spermaceti and mercury. The cream,

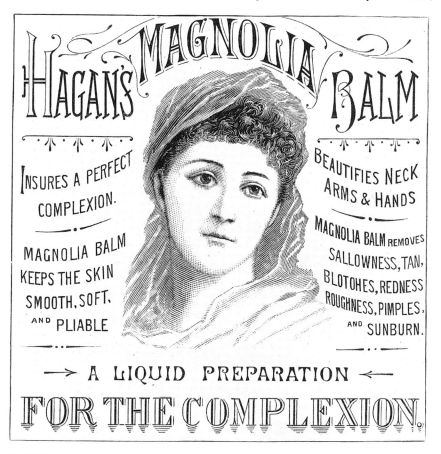

An 1890s advertisement for Hagan's Magnolia Balm, one of many complexion-improving products touted during the Victorian era. (Advertisement for Hagan's Magnolia Balm, 1890s. Wellcome Library, London. Creative Commons Attribution 4.0 International Public License)

when mixed, was pure white and could be scented with (among other things) rose or orange flower water, oil of bergamot or lavender, or vanilla and ambergris.

Blemishes

Victorians believed that pimples were merely the body's way of expelling 'injurious matter' that would otherwise cause ill health. To suppress these skin eruptions was considered to be dangerous. According to Mrs Walker:

> *'The ordinary means which are employed to remove these specks, are remedies which, by their astringent action on the skin, drive back the injurious matter which nature more wisely endeavours to throw out. The least dangerous consequence of this perversion of natural action, is a state of langour a hundred times worse than the superficial and trifling defects which females are so eager to avoid.'*

Blackheads, on the other hand, were directly linked to cosmetic paints, smoke, dirt, and dust, and 'sleeping with the face under the counterpane.' Mrs Walker declares blackheads to be 'as obstinate as they are offensive'. She advises that:

> *'A sponge, or very soft brush, with a little soap, will, in general, by frequent and gentle rubbing, gradually remove them. The face must be washed afterwards, and the operation repeated every morning. If, in spite of this, the specks remain, the only means left is to extract them by pressing them with the two forefingers, which causes neither pain nor inflammation, and at most merely produces a trifling redness for ten minutes.'*

Extraction was not as straightforward a process, however, as some Victorians believed that the gunk which came out was an actual worm. The *Handbook of the Toilette* states:

> *'On the skin being pressed, the bits of coagulated lymph will come from it in a vermicular form. They are vulgarly called "flesh-worms," many ignorant persons supposing them to be living creatures.'*

Various cosmetic washes and spot treatments were available to cure blemishes; however, Freeling warns against 'nostrums such as *Gowland's Lotion*,' claiming that 'all repellent cosmetics are highly dangerous'. To support his claim, he gives several examples of ladies who attempted to treat a pimple only to end up crippled or dead:

> *'Mrs. S, being much troubled with pimples, applied an alum poultice to her face, which was soon followed by a stroke of the palsy, and terminated in her*

death. Mrs. L applied to her face, for pimples, a quack nostrum, supposed to be some preparation of lead. Soon after, she was seized with epileptic fits, which ended in palsy, and caused her death. Mr. Y applied a preparation of lead to his nose, to remove pimples, and it brought on palsy on one side of his face. Miss W, an elegant young lady of about twenty years of age, applied a cosmetic lotion to her face, to remove the "small red pimple." This produced inflammation of the liver, which it required repeated bleeding, with medicine, to remove. As soon as the inflammation was subdued, the pimples reappeared.'

These extreme warnings had little effect on the sales of *Gowland's Lotion*. Despite being poisonous, it remained one of the most popular cosmetic treatments in the Victorian era. *Beeton's Dictionary of Practical Recipes and Every-Day Information*, published in 1871, even provided the following general recipe for making Gowland's Lotion at home:

'Ingredients: 1 ½ gr. of bichloride of mercury and 1 oz. of emulsion of bitter almonds. Mix these thoroughly, and apply the lotion when required with a piece of soft sponge. The bichloride of mercury must be used with care, as it is a poison.'

Sun Damage and Skin Whiteners

Victorian ladies strived for a smooth, white complexion, unmarred by blemishes, freckles, or a suntan. This meant protecting oneself against the elements with hats, veils, and parasols. As Freeling states:

'Of all the effects that exposure of the skin to the air or sun produces, the most disagreeable is that called freckles or tan.'

If, despite one's efforts at prevention, freckles or a tan still managed to make their appearance, there were various treatments available. *Gowland's Lotion* was almost always recommended, as were lemon juice and strawberry water, which were believed to naturally lighten the skin. There were recipes for spot treatments, with ingredients such as turpentine and tincture of benzoin. There were also commercial skin whiteners like *Beetham's Glycerine and Cucumber* and *Aspinall's Neigeline* which, by the end of the century, promised to be 'absolutely non-poisonous'.

For sunburn or 'sun scorch,' Mrs Walker advises washing the face and affected areas every evening with 'new milk, cream, or skimmed milk'. While *Beeton's Dictionary of Practical Recipes and Every-Day Information* recommends an emulsion of blanched, bitter almonds.

Wrinkle Reducers

According to some lady's magazines, beauty books, and health journals, wrinkles in the skin could be attributed to excessive leanness. Still others informed their readers that wrinkles were the product of a negative attitude or sour disposition. For the former, ladies were advised to 'endeavour to acquire plumpness',[68] while for the latter, ladies were directed to counteract the lines etched by negativity with lines of cheerfulness. As the 1898 edition of *Good Health* explains:

> *'The vertical wrinkles of frowns must be smoothed out by the horizontal wrinkles of benevolence and charity. The down-in-the-mouth expression of despair and chronic blues must be antagonized by the countenance-lifting emotions of good cheer. In other words, the hypochondriac must smile, and smile hard, smile with all his might.'*

For some ladies, this advice was not at all practical. They resorted instead to creams and treatments, many of which were based on word of mouth. In her 1858 book *The Arts of Beauty; Or, Secrets of a Lady's Toilet with Hints to Gentlemen on the Art of Fascinating*, the famous nineteenth century beauty Lola Montez informs her readers that:

> *'The celebrated Madam Vestris used to sleep every night with her face plastered up with a kind of paste to ward off the threatening wrinkles, and keep her charming complexion from fading.'*

The recipe for this wrinkle reducing face plaster included eggs whites, alum, and sweet almond oil which were blended together to form a paste. Montez states that when 'spread upon a silk or muslin mask, and worn at night' this paste would not only prevent wrinkles, but also keep the complexion fair and stop loose muscles from sagging.

Some Victorian ladies preferred to steer clear of alum paste or other potentially dangerous wrinkle remedies. Instead, they resorted to facial massage as a means of combating their wrinkles. Fletcher's 1899 book outlines a thorough facial massage regime, complete with illustrations, claiming that:

> *'Massage will in time strengthen the muscles so that the lines will be effaced.'*

Depilatories and Hair Removal

On occasion, a Victorian lady had to deal with unwanted facial hair. Remedies for this troublesome problem ranged from the fairly benign (and probably useless) to the shockingly extreme. At the safer end of the spectrum, the *Book of Health and Beauty* recommends using parsley water, acacia juice, nut oil, 'the gum of ivy,' or 'the juice of the milk-thistle.' These remedies were thought to prevent hair growth.

If these milder methods did not work, one might resort to 'muriatic acid,' diluted or in its concentrated form.

If the stubborn facial hair still persisted, a Victorian lady could always depend on a depilatory made of quick lime to eradicate it completely. Unfortunately, lime was highly corrosive to the skin and using it on the face was a risky business. Despite this danger, recipes for lime depilatories abounded, some of which included arsenic and other lethal substances.

Extreme Skin Care Methods

One might argue that basic Victorian skin care was already extreme and, considering that everyday recipes called for arsenic, mercury, and lime, one would not be wrong. However, there were even more extreme methods of treating the skin. One of these, described as a 'rejuvenating treatment,' involved the use of iodine. As Fletcher relates:

> 'It is a peeling process of the most agonizing sort. After the raw surface heals from four to eight days – the complexion is in some cases very fair and lovely, but as expressionless as a wax doll's; and for months afterward the faintest breath of wind or a touch of the softest cloth in bathing the face causes the most exquisite torture. In a few months after taking this treatment, the sensitive skin commences to show thousands of criss-cross lines, which gradually deepen, till it resembles the shriveled surface of prematurely plucked fruit.'

Victorian ladies also used steam and electricity as a means of treating the skin. Toward the end of the century, steam was applied to the face via a portable vapour-lamp. It was used to open the pores and clear the complexion of acne. While electricity, when properly administered by a 'medical electrician,' was believed to stimulate and energize the nerves and muscles, to promote 'cellular nutrition,' and to quicken the circulation.[69]

Women desperate for youth and beauty were willing to try most anything to keep their skin looking young. Montez relates stories of ladies who flocked to drink the water at arsenic springs, a practice which is said to have imparted 'a transparent whiteness' to their skin. She also claims to have known fashionable ladies in Paris who bound their faces up every night with slices of raw beef in order to prevent wrinkles and to bestow 'a youthful freshness and brilliancy to the complexion.'

Applying raw meat to the face as a means of beautifying the skin was not unheard of during the Victorian era. Some believed that a lacklustre complexion was a result of the skin being starved. The solution was to 'feed the starved tissues' by means of thin slices of raw beef or veal.[70] Even the Empress Elisabeth of Austria was known to sleep in a face mask lined with raw veal in order to preserve her jealously guarded youth and beauty.

Chapter 15

Victorian Cosmetics

*'Ladies of the present day, not content with the gifts of nature, often endeavor
to improve and patch up the faults and imperfections of their complexions
by artificial means.'*

Godey's Lady's Book, 1869.

Attitudes toward cosmetics in the nineteenth century were notoriously negative. Queen Victoria herself denounced make-up as being 'impolite' and mid-century magazines like the *Saturday Evening Review* declared that cosmetics were 'insincere' and 'a form of lying'.[71] Even more damning, to most Victorians, makeup was believed to be the province of only two classes of women; actresses and prostitutes. As such, most ladies considered the very idea of painting their faces to be abhorrent. Nevertheless, cosmetics such as cheek rouge, tinted lip salve, and face powder gradually managed to work their way into the beauty routines of even the most respectable women. For those countless ladies who suffered from imperfections (both real and imagined), cosmetic assistance was, ultimately, too powerful a temptation to resist.

Face Powder

Even those Victorian ladies who shunned colour cosmetics were known to occasionally indulge in a light dusting of face powder. One of the most widely advertised brands was Saunders's Face Powder. It was available in both pure white and in 'a most delicate roseate hue' which was purported to impart 'a pleasing and healthful appearance' to the complexion.[72] Saunders's Face Powder had numerous competitors in the form of face powders which claimed to be made of everything from ground pearls to the finest French talc. In reality, Victorian face powders were often comprised of zinc powder or bismuth blended with chalk or carbonate of lime.

Starch was another popular component of Victorian era facial powders. It could be used either plain or mixed with orris powder. When this mixture was 'perfumed with essential oils,' it was known as 'violet powder,' a product which was considered to be 'one of the least injurious cosmetics'.[73] Perfumed face powders

J. TOUZEAU SAUNDERS, Perfumer, 143, Oxford St., London.

FOR THE

COMPLEXION

SAUNDERS'S FACE POWDER,
OR BLOOM OF NINON.

A most delicate preparation for beautifying the Complexion; free from anything that can injure the Skin.

The Face Powder, which has a most delicate roseate hue, imparts to the Face a pleasing and healthful appearance, and is preferable to all other preparations for preserving and clearing the Complexion.

An advertisement for Saunders's face powder. (*The Chemists' Annual List*, London: John Sanger & Sons, 1872)

were often tinted in shades of delicate pink or rose. The *Book of Health* describes one such powder comprised of chalk, starch, and oxide of zinc which was 'coloured with carmine and scented with rose'. When applied over a fresh application of cold cream, these flesh-coloured powders produced an effect which was not too dissimilar from a modern-day foundation.

In addition to commercially produced powders, beauty books and books of household management contained various recipes for face powder which could be easily made at home. In his 1889 *Practical Hand-Book of Toilet Preparations and Their Uses*, Joseph Begy provides a recipe for flesh-tinted French powder which he claims is 'equal to any French preparation in the market'. The recipe includes zinc oxide, starch, white French chalk, white clay, orrisroot, bitter almonds, sweet orange, rose geranium, and carmine to provide the colour. Once prepared, the powder could be applied with a puff or a chamois to the arms and neck. Begy also includes a recipe for 'complexion powder,' suitable to be used on the face. The preparation contains equal parts of finely pulverized white talc and chalk combined with several drops of Otto of Roses.

Though many facial powders were colourless, it was still possible to overdo them. Ladies who used excessive face powder were as much subject to criticism as those who used too much lip colour or rouge. This fact is exemplified by a humorous exchange published in the 24 October 1900 edition of the *Dundee Evening Post*:

> *"'Doesn't Isabel use a good deal of face powder?"*
> *"Face powder! She ought to belong to the Plasterer's Union."'*

Cheek Rouge

Despite the negative connotations of face paint and other cosmetics, most Victorian beauty books contained at least one recipe for lip or cheek rouge which a lady could use to add a bit of subtle colour to her complexion. These were natural recipes, with the red colouring generally derived from either the cochineal insect or the alkanet root. In his 1846 book *An Easy Introduction to Chemistry*, George Sparkes describes the cochineal as 'a dried insect, which, when powdered, yields a brilliant colour both to water and to alcohol'. The cochineal insect was the basis of carmine, an ingredient which is still used today to colour many varieties of red lipstick and blush.

One of the most well-known brands of cheek rouge from the eighteenth and nineteenth centuries was Circassian Bloom. Also marketed as Bloom of Circassia, it was regularly featured in Victorian era newspaper advertisements alongside other luxurious sounding beauty products like Peach Blossom Cream and Alabaster Liquid. It was also frequently mentioned in eighteenth and nineteenth century fiction, including short stories in magazines and popular comic verses. Perhaps the most quoted of these verses is by the English poet George Crabbe who mentions Circassian Bloom in his 1785 poem, *The Newspaper*. It reads in part:

> *'Come, faded Belles, who would their Youth renew,*
> *And learn the wonders of Olympian dew;*
> *Restore the Roses that begin to faint,*
> *Not think celestial washes, vulgar Paint:*
> *Your former Features, Airs, and Arts assume,*
> *Circassian Virtues, with Circassian Bloom.'*

Circassian Bloom was first advertised during the eighteenth century. A typical advert, as seen in a 1772 edition of *London's Public Advertiser,* begins by declaring that 'Circassians are the most beautiful Women in the World'. To enhance their beauty, the advert states that Circassian ladies have long been accustomed to using a 'liquid bloom' to bring colour to their cheeks. An enterprising Englishman claims to have duplicated the secret of this liquid bloom via an extract from a Circassian vegetable. The resulting liquid was reportedly superior to any other rouge on the market. According to the advertisement:

> *'It instantly gives a rose Hue to the Cheeks not to be distinguished from the lively and animated Bloom of rural Beauty; nor will it come off by Perspiration, or the Use of a Handkerchief.'*

Circassian Bloom continued to be used well into the Victorian era. It was often applied lightly with a hare's foot or swan's-down puff. But however faint the application, among women of good breeding, cheek rouge continued to be viewed as an especially vulgar product. Some publications even went so far as to compare the ruddy cheeks produced by liquid or powder rouge to the ruddy cheeks produced by excessive drink.

Even if a lady avoided the vulgar temptation of Circassian Bloom, it did not necessarily follow that her complexion was rouge free. There were countless methods for staining the cheeks, including strawberry juice, crushed geranium leaves, and rubbing one's cheeks with a red-coloured flannel. There were also many recipes for homemade rouge made from ingredients which were gentler on the skin than the lead, bismuth, and arsenic which featured heavily in the popular cosmetic preparations of the early nineteenth century. Homemade rouge was preferable for other reasons as well. By mixing her rouge herself, a lady could make subtle adjustments to the colour, thus resulting in a much more natural looking shade of rose, pink, or peach on her cheeks.

For ladies wishing to make their own cheek colour, the 1883 edition of *Beeton's Domestic Recipe Book* provides several recipes for rouge in which the red hue is derived from carmine powder or tincture of cochineal. Alternatively, an 1870 edition of *Harper's Bazaar* recommends adding carmine or flakes of indigo to a base recipe of the popular complexion wash known as Milk of Roses. The recipe calls for oil of almonds, oil of tartar, and rose-water, a mixture to which carmen or indigo could be added to make shades ranging from 'deep black-rose crimson' to the more delicate 'soft Greuze tints.'

Despite the availability of recipes for liquid and powder rouge or for commercial products like Circassian Bloom, cheek rouge would never be fully acceptable in the Victorian era. Instead, beauty books and magazines urged women to cultivate good health and the naturally rosy cheeks resulting from fresh air and exercise. For those women determined to assist nature, beauty experts recommended a light hand. As *Harper's Bazaar* wisely advises:

> 'If she must resort to artificial beauty, let her be artistic about it, and not lay on paint as one would furniture polish rubbed in with rags.'

Lip Rouge and Lip Salve

For most of the Victorian era, ladies who wished to add a rosy hue to their lips relied on lip rouge or tinted lip salve. Like cheek rouge, red lip salve was fairly easy for a lady – or her maid – to make up at home. In the 1840s and 1850s, Victorian ladies made red lip salve using suet and lard boiled together with alkanet chips to produce 'a fine deep red' colour.[74] Later recipes, such as the one provided in the 1892 book *Perfumes and their Preparation*, called for oil of almonds, wax, spermaceti, and alkanet root which, when blended together, promised to impart a 'beautiful red colour' to the lips.

A VICTORIAN LADY'S GUIDE TO FASHION AND BEAUTY

Though recipes for red lip rouge and red lip salve abounded in lady's magazines and beauty books, lip colour – like cheek rouge – was never entirely respectable. Natural beauty remained the ideal for the better part of the nineteenth century. By the late Victorian era, however, attitudes toward cosmetics were gradually beginning to change. This was largely as a result of actresses, like Sarah Bernhardt, who routinely wore makeup in public. In addition, the advent of industrialization spurred on the production of commercial cosmetics. Victorian ladies were now able to order their cosmetics through the post or purchase them at the chemist shop or druggist. Soon, the cosmetics industry was flourishing in both England and America, and as *Harper's Bazaar* states:

> *'The time has gone by when it was a matter of church discipline if a woman painted her face or wore powder. Nor is it any serious reflection on her moral character if she go abroad with her complexion made up in the forenoon, however it may call her taste in question. All who paint their faces and look forth at their windows are not visited with hard names, else the parlor of every house on the side-Streets of New York might have its Jezebel waiting the dinner-hour and the return of masculine admirers.'*

FINISHING TOUCHES: MADAME SARAH BERNHARDT IN HER DRESSING-ROOM

Actresses like Sarah Bernhardt helped to make cosmetics acceptable for Victorian women to wear. (Finishing Touches, Madame Sarah Bernhardt in her Dressing Room, The *Graphic*, 21 July 1894. © British Library Board)

Perfumes

A Victorian lady was not known for wearing an excess of scent. Nevertheless, perfumes were as much a part of a Victorian woman's beauty regime as hair and skin care. These perfumes were generally simpler than the ones we know today and consisted, in large part, of florals and other botanicals, such as rose, violet, bergamot, lemon, and lavender. They were rarely applied directly to the skin. Instead, Victorian perfumes were used to scent handkerchiefs, gloves, and clothing, and even as a fragrant additive in cosmetic products like hair pomade or lip salve. Some fragrances were nineteenth century mainstays.

At the beginning of the Victorian era, the predominant scent was *Eau de Cologne*. Consisting of a base of neroli oil (an oil derived from orange blossoms and flowers from the bitter orange tree), *Eau de Cologne* had risen to popularity during the eighteenth century. Advertisements of the period describe it as being made from 'the finest, strongest, and most exquisite flowers the earth can produce'.[75] Though chiefly used as a perfume, it was also valued for its purported medicinal properties. Many varieties were made with spirits of grape or corn, a fact which led some Victorian ladies to use *Eau de Cologne* as a stimulant. The 27 September 1894 edition of the *St. James's Gazette* reports:

> *'One hears, of course, from time to time of eau de Cologne being used as a "pick-me-up," and even as an intoxicant, especially by women whose sense of shame prevents them from purchasing the gin, brandy, or whisky with which they would otherwise gratify their inclinations.'*

Natural scents like florals, herbals, and oils derived from the rinds of citrus fruits were also very popular throughout the Victorian era. As an 1840 edition of the *Saturday Magazine* states:

> *'Herbs, drugs, and flowers, are made to yield their aromatic odours for our use. Among the former we may mention marjoram, sage, thyme, lavender, &c., while of drugs, frankincense, mace, cloves, benzoin, storax, and many others, are held in great esteem. Orange-flowers, jonquils, jessamine, roses, violets, and other fragrant flowers, are also largely employed, and thus, by a judicious use of some of these various essences, we may impart to our dwellings or our dress, the delightful odours of our favourite flowers, at any period of the year."*

One of the most well-known floral scents was the famous *Otto of Roses* (also known as rose otto or attar of roses). Made from the petals of the 'hundred-leaved rose' – or *rosa centifolia* – the *Saturday Magazine* calls *Otto of Roses* 'the most costly of all the perfumes and the most powerful'. Though its title as the most expensive perfume would soon be eclipsed by the fashionably complex scents of the 1880s and 1890s, *Otto of Roses* would remain a favourite fragrance throughout the Victorian era and into the twentieth century.

By the end of the Victorian era, the advent of inexpensive synthetic fragrances resulted in perfumes being available to an even wider range of women. Wishing to distance themselves from the perfumes used by the lower classes, wealthy ladies began to demand more complex, and as yet unsynthesized, perfumes. This demand did not go unanswered. By the 1890s, single scent perfumes had given way to fashionable perfumes made of complicated combinations of spice oils and animal essences, like musk, ambergris, and civet. Animal essences were heavier than botanical scents and their fragrance lasted far longer.

When it came to purchasing perfumes, Victorian women had a wide variety of choices. At the beginning of the era, there were approximately forty pharmacists and perfumers working in London alone – the same amount as in Paris at that time.[76] Not only did these perfumers sell *Eau de Cologne* and other popular fragrances of the day, they frequently came up with their own perfumes as well. For example, in 1861, the House of Guerlain created *Eau de Cologne Imperiale* for the Empress Eugénie, wife of Napoleon III and, in 1872, the London perfumer Penhaligon's launched the fragrance *Hammam Bouquet*, a perfume which they still sell today.

The most fashionable perfumes of the late Victorian era were sold in exquisite bottles made of crystal or cut glass inside of which were small vials or tubes which held a few drops of costly perfume. At the end of the century, scent bottles with the stopper shaped like a flower were a particular novelty. One of the most expensive of this variety is reported to have been made with a stopper in the form of a pink rose. The heart of the rose was comprised of a pink topaz and the petals were made of pink enamel which glistened with 'diamond dew drops.'[77]

The End of an Era

On 22 January 1901, Queen Victoria died at the age of eighty-one. The news of her death was met with a profound sense of grief and distress. The 23 January 1901 edition of the *St. James's Gazette* reports that, upon learning that their sovereign had died, 'a pregnant overwhelming sense of isolation' descended over the 'stupefied' public. The Victorian era – a more than sixty year period which had been marked by not only dramatic changes in women's fashion, but also by significant advances in industry, medicine, and gender equality – had officially come to an end.

The nation fell into mourning for their deceased queen. At the same time, they were looking forward to a brighter, more promising future. On 9 August 1902, they celebrated the coronation of a new sovereign. Queen Victoria's eldest son, Prince Albert Edward, was crowned King Edward VII by the Archbishop of Canterbury in a lavish ceremony at Westminster Abbey. The Edwardian era had begun.

Much like the Victorian era, the Edwardian era would be distinguished by changes in industry, law, and global politics. However, when it came to fashion, Edwardian ladies had already reaped the benefits of their trailblazing Victorian forebears. The practical, no-nonsense dresses and sportswear of the 1890s were fully embraced by a generation of women who were on the move – in more ways than one. They travelled by rail, omnibus, and motorcar, they visited music halls and picture palaces, and, most notably, they continued to fight for women's equality, as well as for the right to vote.

As the decades marched on, hemlines would rise and fall, corsets would be discarded in favour of brassieres, and hats would first grow larger, then shrink smaller, and soon disappear altogether. But despite the many advances that were still to come, the dramatic evolution of women's fashion that took place during the reign of Queen Victoria would never again be replicated. Today, the Victorian era still stands as one of the most significant, and ultimately unforgettable, periods in women's fashion history.

Sources

Aberdeen Evening Express (Aberdeenshire, Scotland), 21 February, 1888. © British Library Board.

ALDRICH, Elizabeth. *From the Ballroom to Hell: Grace and Folly in Nineteenth-Century Dance*. Evanston: Northwestern University Press, 1991.

The American Journal of Obstetrics and Diseases of Women and Children, Volume XXXIII. New York: William Wood & Company, 1896.

ANDERSON, Nancy Fix. *The Sporting Life: Victorian Sports and Games*. Oxford: ABC-CLIO, 2010.

The Art Interchange, Vols. 14-17. New York: Art Interchange Co., 1885.

Arthur's Home Magazine, Vol. XXIII. Philadelphia: T. S. Arthur, 1864.

Arthur's Home Magazine, Vol. XLIII. Philadelphia: T. S. Arthur, 1875.

ASKINSON, George William. *Perfumes and Their Preparation*. London: N. W. Henley, 1892.

BACLAWSKI, *Karen. The Guide to Historic Costume*. New York: Drama Book Publishers, 1995.

Bath Chronicle and Weekly Gazette (Somerset, England), 23 June 1881 and 29 August 1901. © British Library Board.

BAYARD, Madame. *The Art of Beauty; or Lady's Companion to the Boudoir*. London: Weldon & Co., 1876.

Bazaar Exchange and Mart, and Journal of the Household, Vol. XLVIII. London: L. Upcott Gill, 1893.

Beauty: Its Attainment and Preservation. New York: Butterick Publishing Company, 1892.

BEETON, Isabella. Ed. *Beeton's Book of Household Management*. London: Farrar, Straus, and Giroux, 1861.

BEETON, Isabella. *Beeton's Domestic Recipe Book*. London: Ward, Lock, & Co., 1883.

BEETON, Samuel Orchart. *Beeton's Dictionary of Practical Recipes and Every-Day Information*. London: Ward, Lock, and Tyler: 1871.

Beeton's Young Englishwoman. London: Ward, Lock, and Tyler, 1875.

BEGY, Joseph A. *Practical Hand-Book of Toilet Preparations and Their Uses*. New York: WM. L. Allison, 1889.

Bow Bells Weekly. London: J. Dicks, 1866-1874

Belfast News-Letter, (Antrim, Northern Ireland), 4 November 1875. © British Library Board.

Blackwood's Lady's Magazine. London: A. H. Blackwood and Page, 1841-1857

Bizarre, Vol. V. Philadelphia: 1854.

SOURCES

BLANCO, José. *Clothing and Fashion: American Fashion from Head to Toe.* Santa Barbara: ABC-CLIO, 2015.

The Book of Fashionable Life: Comprising the Etiquette of the Drawing Room, Dining Room, and Ball Room. London: Hugh Cunningham, 1845.

The Book of Health and Beauty. London: Joseph Thomas, 1837.

The British Almanac and Companion. London: Company of Stationers, 1877.

BUCHANAN, Paul D. *The American Women's Rights Movement: A Chronology of Events and Opportunities from 1600 to 2008.* Boston: Braden Books, 2009.

The Cambridge History of Western Textiles, Vols. I and II. Edited by D. T. Jenkins. Cambridge: Cambridge University Press, 2003.

CARLIN, William. *Old Doctor Carlin's Recipes.* Boston: Locke Publishing, 1881.

Carlisle Journal (Cumbria, England), 15 February 1840. © British Library Board.

Cassell's Family Magazine. London: Cassell Petter & Galpin, 1874-1896.

Cassell's Household Guide, Vol. I. London: Cassell, Petter, and Galpin, 1873.

The Chemists' Annual List. London: John Sanger & Son, 1870.

Chambers Journal, Vol. 61, Issue 1. London: W. & R. Chambers, 1884.

CHURCH, Ella Rodman. *The Home Needle.* New York: D. Appleton and Co., 1882.

Clothing and Fashion: American Fashion from Head to Toe. Edited by José Blanco. Santa Barbara: ABC-Clio, 2015.

The Clothier and Furnisher, Vol. XIV. New York: Root & Tinker, 1884.

The Columbian Lady's and Gentleman's Magazine. New York: Israel Post, 1846.

COOLEY, Arnold James. *Instructions and Cautions Respecting the Selection and Use of Perfumes, Cosmetics, and Other Toilet Articles.* Philadelphia: J. B. Lippincott & Co, 1873.

COOLEY, Arnold James. *The Toilet and Cosmetic Arts in Ancient and Modern Times.* London: Robert Hardwicke, 1866.

The Cosmopolitan, Vol. XXI. New York: Schlicht & Field, 1896

The Court, Lady's Magazine, Monthly Critic and Museum, Vol. X. Dobbs & Co., 1842.

COURTAIS, Georgine de. *Women's Hats, Headdresses, and Hairstyles.* Mineola: Dover Publications, 1973.

CRABBE, George. *The Poetical Works of George Crabbe.* London: George Routledge and Sons, 1858.

CUNNINGTON, Cecil Willett. *English Women's Clothing in the Nineteenth Century.* London: Faber and Faber Ltd., 1939.

CUNNINGTON, C. Willett. *Fashion and Women's Attitudes in the Nineteenth Century.* New York: Dover Publications, 2003.

The Dangers of Crinoline, Steel Hoops, &c. Pamphlet. London: G. Vickers, 1858.

DE BURGH, Edward Morgan Alborough. *Elisabeth, Empress of Austria, a Memoir.* London: Hutchinson & Co., 1899.

The Delineator. New York: Butterick Publishing Co., 1876-1901.

DICK, William Brisbane. *The Encyclopedia of Practical Receipts.* New York: Dick & Fitzgerald, 1884.

The Domestic Monthly: An Illustrated Magazine of Fashion, Literature, and the Fine Arts, Vol. XXIII. New York: Blake and Company, 1885.

Dundee Evening Telegraph (Angus, Scotland), 5 September, 1885. © British Library Board.

Dundee Evening Telegraph (Angus, Scotland), 17 April 1899. © British Library Board.

The Eclectic Magazine, Vol. VII. New York: Leavitt, Trow, & Co., 1846.

Englishwoman's Domestic Magazine. London: S. O. Beeton, 1852-1879.

The Era Formulary: 5000 Formulas for Druggists. Detroit: D. O. Haynes & Company, 1893.

EWING, Elizabeth. *Fashion in Underwear: From Babylon to Bikini Briefs.* Mineola: Dover Publications, 1971.

EYRE, Mary. *A Lady's Walk in the South of France.* London: R. Bently, 1865.

Fashion: The Definitive History of Costume and Style. New York: DK Publishing, 2012.

FLETCHER, Ella Adelia. *The Woman Beautiful.* New York: W. M. Young & Co., 1899.

Frank Leslie's Illustrated Newspaper, Volumes 69-71. New York: Frank Leslie, 1890.

FREELING, Arthur. *Gracefulness: A Few Words upon Form and Features.* London: George Routledge, 1845.

FROST, Sarah Annie. *The Art of Dressing Well: A Complete Guide to Economy, Style, and Propriety of Costume.* New York: Dick & Fitzgerald, 1870.

Gardeners Monthly and Horticulturist, Vol. XVIII. Philadelphia: Charles H. Marot, 1876.

The Gentleman's Magazine of Fashion and Costumes de Paris et Londres, Vol. 29. London: Simpkin, Marshall & Co., 1877

The Globe (London, England), 31 December 1881. © British Library Board.

The Globe (London, England), 6 April 1899. © British Library Board.

Gloucestershire Echo (Gloucestershire, England), 19 September 1887. © British Library Board.

The Glories of Crinoline. London: Dalton and Lucy, 1866.

Godey's Lady's Book. Philadelphia: Louis A. Godey, 1842-1899.

Golf Illustrated, Vol. V. London, 1900.

Good Health: A Journal of Hygiene, Vol. XXXIII. Battle Creek: Good Health Co., 1898.

Good Health, Vol. XXVII. London: Good Health Publishing Company, 1892.

Good Health, Vol. XXX. London: Good Health Publishing Company, 1895.

Good Housekeeping. Springfield: Clark W. Bryan Company, 1885-1901.

Graham's American Monthly Magazine of Literature, Art, and Fashion, Volume 47. Philadelphia: Abraham H. See, 1855

GRAND, Sarah. 'The New Aspect of the Woman in Question.' *The North American Review, Volume CLVIII.* Boston: University of Northern Iowa, 1894.

The Graphic (London, England), 17 August 1895. © British Library Board.

The Graphic (London, England), 30 May 1896. © British Library Board.

Greenwood Encyclopedia of Clothing through World History, Vol. III. Edited by Jill Condra. London: Greenwood Press, 2008.

GROOM, Nigel. *The New Perfume Handbook.* London: Blackie Academic and Professional, 1997.

Hall's Journal of Health, Vol. 41. New York: Hall's Journal of Health Pub., 1894.

The Handbook of the Toilette. London: W. S. Orr and Co., 1841.

Harper's Bazaar. New York: Hearst Corporation, 1870-1887.

HARRIS, Kristina. *Authentic Victorian Fashion Patterns.* New York: Dover Publications, 1999.

SOURCES

HOCK, Leichter. Ed. *Crinoline in its Bissextile Phases.* London: Robert Hardwicke, 1864.

Home Notes, London, Vol. V. London: C. Arthur Pearson, 1895.

Household Words. London: Charles Dickens & Evans, 1883-1885.

The Jewelers' Circular and Horological Review, Vol. 15. New York: Jewelers' Circular Publishing Company, 1884.

The Illustrated American, Vol. 7. New York: Illustrated American Publising, 1891.

The Illustrated Exhibitor, Part I. London: John Cassell, 1851.

The Illustrated News of the World. London: Emily Faithful, 1863.

KARR, Elizabeth. *The American Horsewoman.* Boston: Houghton, Mifflin and Co., 1884.

Kendal Mercury (Cumbria, England), 06 January 1866. © British Library Board.

KINGSFORD, Anna Bonus. *Health, Beauty and the Toilet: Letters to Ladies from a Lady Doctor.* London: Frederick Warne and Co., 1886.

KORTSCH, Christine Bayles. *Dress Culture in Late Victorian Women's Fiction.* New York: Routledge, 2009.

The Ladies' Cabinet of Fashion, Music, and Romance, Vol. V. London: Geo. Henderson, 1841.

The Ladies' Cabinet of Fashion, Music, & Romance, Vol. III. London: Geo. Henderson, 1847.

The Ladies' Companion and Monthly Magazine. London: Rodgerson and Tuxford, 1851-1866.

The Ladies Home Journal. Philadelphia: Curtis Publishing Co., 1889-1901.

The Ladies' Monthly Magazine. London: Simpkin, Marshall, & Co., 1869-1875.

The Ladies Pocket Book of Etiquette. London: George Bell, 1840.

The Lady's Companion, Vol. XVII. New York: William Snowden, 1842.

The Lady's Home Magazine, Vol. XI. Philadelphia: T. S. Arthur, 1858.

The Lady's Magazine and Museum, Vol. XI. London: Dobbs & Co., 1837.

LAWRENCE, Sir Walter Roper. *The Valley of Kashmir.* London: Asian Educational Services, 1895.

Le Follet, Journal Du Grand Monde. London : E. Minister & Son, 1863.

Le Moniteur de la Mode. London: L'Office du Moniteur, 1851-1852.

Leeds Intelligencer (West Yorkshire, England), 2 July 1859. © British Library Board.

LEONARD, Charles Henri. *The Hair: Its Growth, Care, Diseases and Treatments.* Detroit: Illustrated Medical Journal, 1879.

LESCRIBLEUR, V. *The Great Anti-Crinoline League.* London: Wyman & Sons, 1883.

LESLIE, Eliza. *Miss Leslie's Lady's New Receipt-Book: A Useful Guide for Large or Small Families.* Philadelphia: A. Hart, 1850.

LICHTENFELD, Joseph. *Principles of Modern Hairdressing.* London: Joseph Lichtenfeld, 1881.

Life, Volume XXXIV. New York: Life Office, 1899.

The London and Paris Ladies' Magazine of Fashion. London: Simpkin, Marshall, and Co., 1851-1854.

The London and Paris Ladies' Magazine of Fashion. London: William Stevens, 1866-1872.

The London and Paris Ladies' Magazine of Fashion, Vol. XLV. London: William Stevens, 1872.

The London and Paris Ladies' Magazine of Fashion, Literature, and Fine Arts, Vol. 58. London: Kent & Co., 1885.

The London Quarterly Review, Vol. XXVII. New York: Leonard Scott, 1846.

London Society Magazine. London: William Clowes and Sons, 1868-1881.

MACINTYRE, John. *The Whole Golf Book.* Naperville: Sourcebooks, 2005.

MARSH, Madeleine. *Compacts and Cosmetics: Beauty from Victorian Times to the Present Day.* Barnsley: Remember When, 2009.

MILLER, Michael Barry. *The Bon Marché: Bourgeois Culture and the Department Store, 1869-1920.* Princeton: Princeton University Press, 1981.

MILLER, Scott. *Historical Dictionary of Modern Japanese Literature and Theater.* Plymouth: Scarecrow Press, 2009.

Milliner and Dressmaker and Warehouseman's Gazette. London: Adolphe Goubaud and Son, 1870.

MONTEZ, Lola. *The Arts of Beauty; Or, Secrets of a Lady's Toilet with Hints to Gentlemen on the Art of Fascinating.* New York: Dick & Fitzgerald, 1858.

Morning Chronicle (London, England), 16 September 1851. © The British Library Board.

Morning Post (London, England), 21 April 1855. © British Library Board.

Morning Post (London, England), 28 December 1870. © British Library Board.

MORRIS, Sir Malcolm Alexander. *The Book of Health.* London: Cassell & Co., 1883.

MOSLEY, Stephen. *The Environment in World History.* London: Routledge, 2010.

Myra's Journal of Dress and Fashion. London: Weldon, August 1878.

Myra's Threepenny Journal. London: Coubaud & Son, 1883.

Nelson, Carolyn Christensen, Ed. *A New Woman Reader: Fiction, Articles, and Drama of the 1890s.* Ontario: Broadview Press, 2001.

New Monthly Belle Assemblée. London: Joseph Rogerson, 1834-1870.

North Devon Gazette (Devon, England), 17 September 1901. © British Library Board.

North London News (London, England), 3 May 1884. © British Library Board.

North London News (London, England), 24 April 1886. © British Library Board.

NUDELMAN, Zoya. *The Art of Couture Sewing.* New York: Fairchild Books, 2009.

Official Lawn Tennis Bulletin, Vol. IV. Cambridge: John Wilson and Son, University Press, 1897.

O'DONOGHUE, Mrs Power. *Riding for Ladies, with Hints on the Stable.* London: W. Thacker & Co., 1887.

Once a Month, Vol. IV. London: Griffith, Farran, & Co., 1886.

PALLINGSTON, Jessica. Lipstick: A Celebration of the World's Favorite Cosmetic. New York: St. Martin's Press, 1999.

Party-Giving on Every Scale. London: Frederick Warne & Co., 1880.

PATERSON, T. V. *The Art of Living; or Good Advice for Young and Old.* London: A. J. Barnes & Co., 1885.

People's Medical Journal and Family Physician, Vol. I. London: George Vickers, 1850.

PERROT, Phillipe. *Fashioning the Bourgeoisie.* Princeton: Princeton University Press, 1994.

Peterhead Sentinel and General Advertiser for Buchan District (Aberdeenshire, Scotland), 26 June 1863. © British Library Board.

Peterson's Magazine. Philadelphia: C.J. Peterson, 1853-1882.

SOURCES

PRICE, Julius Mendes. *Dame Fashion.* New York: Scribner and Sons, 1913.

Punch, Vol. 48-49. London: Punch Publications Ltd., 1865.

REED, I. N. *The Ladies' Manual.* New York: I. N. Reed & Co., 1883.

RHIND, Jennifer Peace. *Fragrance and Wellbeing.* Philadelphia: Singing Dragon, 2014.

RIMMEL, Eugene. *The Book of Perfumes.* London: Chapman and Hall, 1865.

The Saturday Magazine, Vol. XV. London: John William Parker, 1840.

Scots Observer, Vol. I. Edinburgh: T & A Constable, 1888-1889.

SCOTT, Clement. *The Wheel of Life: A Few Memories and Recollections.* London: Lawrence Greening, 1897.

The Secret Revealed: How to Acquire Personal Beauty. Chicago: R. S. Peale & Co., 1889.

SELL, Charles. *Chemistry of Fragrances: From Perfumer to Consumer.* Royal Society of Chemistry, 2006.

Sheffield Evening Telegraph (South Yorkshire, England), 25 April 1899. © British Library Board.

Sheffield Weekly Telegraph (South Yorkshire, England), 29 January 1898. © British Library Board.

SHERROW, Victoria. *For Appearance' Sake: The Historical Encyclopedia of Good Looks, Beauty, and Grooming.* Westport: Oryx Press, 2001.

The Shilling Book of Beauty. Cuthbert Bede, Ed. London: J. Blackwood, 1856.

SILVER, Anna Krugovoy. *Victorian Literature and the Anorexic Body.* Cambridge: Cambridge University Press, 2004.

The Sketch: A Journal of Art and Actuality, Vol. 21. London: Ingram Brothers, 1898.

SPARKES, George. *An Easy Introduction to Chemistry.* London: Wittaker & Co., 1846.

The Speaker, Vol. 20. London: Mather & Crowther, 1899.

St. James's Gazette (London, England), 31 August 1889. © British Library Board.

St. James's Gazette (London, England), 27 September 1894. © British Library Board.

St. James's Gazette (London, England), 23 January 1901. © British Library Board.

Surrey Mirror (Surrey, England), 22 September 1894. © British Library Board.

Sylvia's Book of the Toilet: A Ladies' Guide to Dress and Beauty. London: Ward, Lock, and Co., 1881.

Table Talk. Philadelphia: Table Talk Publishing, 1892-1895.

Tamworth Herald (Staffordshire, England), 01 January 1881. © British Library Board.

THESANDER, Marianne. *The Feminine Ideal.* London: Reaktion Books, 1997.

TORTORA, Phyllis G. *A Survey of Historic Costume.* New York: Fairchild Press, 1989.

Townsend's Monthly Selection of Parisian Costumes. London: Simpkin, Marshall & Co., January 1881.

Truth: A Weekly Journal, Vol. X. London: Wyman & Sons, 1881.

Vick's Monthly Magazine, Vol. I. Rochester: Vick's, 1878.

Victorian and Edwardian Fashion from La Mode Illustrée. Edited by JoAnne Olian. Mineola: Dover Publications, 1998.

Victorian Fashions and Costumes from Harper's Bazar, 1867-1898. Edited by Stella Blum. Mineola: Dover Publications, 1974.

WALKER, Mrs A. *Female Beauty, as Preserved and Improved by Regimen, Cleanliness and Dress.* New York: Scofield and Voorhies, 1840.

Ward and Lock's Home Book: A Domestic Encyclopaedia. London: Ward, Lock, and Co., 1882.

WARD, Maria E. *The Common Sense of Bicycling: Bicycling for Ladies.* New York: Brenano's. 1896.

The Water Cure Journal, Vol. 7-8. New York: Fowlers and Wells, 1849.

Wells Journal (Somerset, England), 25 April 1889. © The British Library Board.

WEST, John. *Maidenhood and Motherhood; or the Phases of a Woman's Life.* Chicago: Law, King, & Law, 1887.

Western Daily Press (Bristol, England), 8 February 1883. © British Library Board.

Western Druggist, Vol. 15. Chicago: G.P. Engelhard & Co., 1893.

WILLIAMS, Jean. *A Contemporary History of Women's Sport, Part One: Sporting Women, 1850-1960.* New York: Routledge, 2014.

WILSON, Sir Erasmus. *Healthy Skin: A Popular Treatise on the Skin and Hair, Their Preservation and Management.* London: J. & A. Churchill, 1872.

The Woman's World. Edited by Oscar Wilde. London: Cassell & Company, 1888-1890.

Wood's Medical and Surgical Monographs, Vol. VIII. New York: William Wood and Co., 1890.

The World of Fashion, and Continental Feuilletons, Vo. II. London: Bell, 1841.

The World of Fashion, and Continental Feuilletons, Vol. 62. London: Simpkin, Marshall, and Co., 1885.

WOSK, Julie. *Women and the Machine: Representations from the Spinning Wheel to the Electronic Age.* Baltimore: JHU Press, 2003.

Wright & Ditson Officially Adopted Lawn Tennis Guide. Boston: Wright & Ditson, 1891.

WYMER, Norman. *Sport in England: A History of Two Thousand Years of Games and Pastimes.* London: Harrap, 1949.

YOKOYAMA, Toshio. *Japan in the Victorian Mind: A Study of Stereotyped Images of a Nation,* 1850-80. London: The Macmillan Press, 1987.

Yorkshire Post and Leeds Intelligencer, (West Yorkshire, England), 6 May 1874. © British Library Board.

Notes

1. Cunnington, C. Willett (1939). *English Women's Clothing in the Nineteenth Century.* London: Faber and Faber Ltd., p. 131.
2. *Greenwood Encyclopedia of Clothing through World History, Vol. III* (2008). Edited by Jill Condra. London: Greenwood Press, p. 47.
3. Buchanan, Paul D (2009). *The American Women's Rights Movement: A Chronology of Events and Opportunities from 1600 to 2008.* Boston: Braden Books, p. 52.
4. Price, Julius Mendes (1913). *Dame Fashion.* New York: Scribner and Sons, p. 126.
5. *Wells Journal* (Somerset, England), 25 April 1889; p. 5. © British Library Board.
6. *Peterhead Sentinel and General Advertiser for Buchan District* (Aberdeenshire, Scotland), 26 June 1863; p. 4. © British Library Board.
7. *Peterson's Magazine, Vol. 64-64* (1873). Philadelphia: C.J. Peterson, p. 81.
8. *Yorkshire Post and Leeds Intelligencer*, (West Yorkshire, England), 6 May 1874; p. 1. © British Library Board.
9. *Belfast News-Letter*, (Antrim, Northern Ireland), 4 November 1875; p. 3. © British Library Board.
10. *Godey's Lady's Book, Vol. 98-99* (1879). Philadelphia: Louis A. Godey, p. 476.
11. *The Nation: A Weekly Journal, Vol. IV* (1869). New York: E. L. Godkin & Co., p. 174.
12. *Globe* (London, England), 31 December 1881; p. 7. © British Library Board
13. *The World of Fashion, and Continental Feuilletons, Vol. 62* (1885). London: Simpkin, Marshall, and Co., p. 8.
14. *The London and Paris Ladies' Magazine of Fashion, Literature, and Fine Arts, Vol. 58* (April, 1885). London: Kent & Co., pp. 2-3.
15. *Aberdeen Evening Express* (Aberdeenshire, Scotland), 21 February, 1888; p. 2. © British Library Board.
16. *Gloucestershire Echo* (Gloucestershire, England), 19 September 1887; p. 3. © British Library Board.
17. *Dundee Evening Telegraph* (Angus, Scotland), 5 September, 1885; p. 2. © British Library Board.
18. *Godey's Lady's Book, Vol. 102-103* (1881), Philadelphia: Louis A. Godey, p. 469.
19. *Peterson's Magazine, Vol. 85-86* (1884), Philadelphia: C.J. Peterson, p. 180.
20. *Dundee Evening Telegraph* (Angus, Scotland), 11 June 1888; p. 3. © British Library Board.
21. *St James's Gazette* (London, England), 31 August 1889; p. 15. © British Library Board.

22. Kortsch, Christine Bayles (2009). *Dress Culture in Late Victorian Women's Fiction.* New York: Routledge, p. 83.
23. *Western Daily Press* (Bristol, England), 8 February 1883; p.3. © British Library Board.
24. *Truth: A Weekly Journal, Vol. X* (1881). London: Wyman & Sons, p. 492.
25. Ibid.
26. Tortora, Phyllis G. (1989). *A Survey of Historic Costume.* New York: Fairchild Press, p. 262.
27. *Dundee Evening Telegraph* (Angus, Scotland), 17 April 1899; p. 4. © British Library Board.
28. *Godey's Lady's Book, Vol. 130* (1895). Philadelphia: Louis A. Godey, p. 555.
29. Ibid.
30. *Bazaar Exchange and Mart, and Journal of the Household, Vol. XLVIII* (1893). London: L. Upcott Gill, p. 986.
31. Ibid.
32. *Godey's Lady's Book, Vol. 132* (1896). Philadelphia: Louis A. Godey, p. 211.
33. Ibid., p. 448.
34. *Hall's Journal of Health, Vol. 41* (1894). New York: Hall's Journal of Health Pub., p. 211.
35. *The Ladies' Monthly Magazine, Vol. 52* (1875). London: Simpkin, Marshall, & Co., p. 1.
36. Cunnington, p. 277.
37. O'Donoghue, Mrs Power (1887). *Riding for Ladies, with Hints on the Stable.* London: W. Thacker & Co., p. 49.
38. Karr, Elizabeth Platt (1884). *The American Horsewoman.* Boston: Houghton, Mifflin and Co., p. 52.
39. Moustache, Vielle (1874). *The Barb and the Bridle: A Handbook of Equitation for Ladies.* London: The Queen Newspaper Office, p. 14
40. *The Columbian Lady's and Gentleman's Magazine* (1846). New York: Israel Post, p. 180.
41. *Cassell's Family Magazine* (1877). London: Cassell Petter & Galpin, p. 626.
42. *Frank Leslie's Illustrated Newspaper, Volumes 69-71* (1890). New York: Frank Leslie, p. 458.
43. Ibid.
44. Wymer, Norman (1949). *Sport in England: A History of Two Thousand Years of Games and Pastimes.* London: Harrap, p. 226.
45. MacIntyre, John (2005). *The Whole Golf Book.* Naperville: Sourcebooks, p. 211
46. Ward, Maria E (1896). *The Common Sense of Bicycling: Bicycling for Ladies.* New York: Brenano's. p. 93.
47. *The Delineator, Vol. 52* (1898). New York: Butterick Publishing Co., p. 48.
48. *Carlisle Journal* (Cumbria, England), 15 February 1840; p. 3 © British Library Board.
49. *Household Words, Vol. VIII (1885).* London: Charles Dickens & Evans, p. 457.
50. Frost, Sarah Annie (1870). The Art of Dressing Well: A Complete Guide to Economy, Style, and Propriety of Costume. New York: Dick & Fitzgerald, p. 93.
51. *The Delineator, Vol. 46* (1895). New York: Butterick Publishing Co., p. 493.
52. Walker, Mrs A (1840). *Female Beauty, as Preserved and Improved by Regimen, Cleanliness and Dress.* New York: Scofield and Voorhies, p. 239.

NOTES

53. Ibid., p. 248.

54. *Wood's Medical and Surgical Monographs, Vol. VIII* (1890). New York: William Wood and Co., p. 422.

55. *Sylvia's Book of the Toilet: A Ladies' Guide to Dress and Beauty* (1881). London: Ward, Lock, and Co., p. 33.

56. Leonard, Charles Henri (1879). *The Hair: Its Growth, Care, Diseases and Treatments.* Detroit: Illustrated Medical Journal, p. 167.

57. Marsh, Madeleine (2009). *Compacts and Cosmetics: Beauty from Victorian Times to the Present Day.* Barnsley: Remember When, p. 28.

58. *Englishwoman's Domestic Magazine, Vol. II* (1853). London: S. O. Beeton, 1853; p. 62.

59. Challamel, Augustin (1882). *The History of Fashion in France.* London: Sampson Low, Marston, Searle, & Riviton, p. 225.

60. Godey's Lady's Book, Vol. XLIV (1852). Philadelphia: Louis A. Godey, p. 521.

61. Godey's Lady's Book, Vol. LXVII (1863). Philadelphia: Louis A. Godey, p. 593.

62. Bayard, Madame (1876). *The Art of Beauty; or Lady's Companion to the Boudoir.* London: Weldon & Co., p. 21.

63. *Myra's Threepenny Journal* (1883). London: Coubaud & Son, p. 124.

64. *Beauty: Its Attainment and Preservation* (1892). New York: Butterick Publishing Company, p. 404.

65. Ibid.

66. *Sheffield Weekly Telegraph* (South Yorkshire, England), 29 January 1898; p. 9. © British Library Board.

67. Carlin, William (1881). *Old Doctor Carlin's Recipes.* Boston: Locke Publishing, p. 477.

68. Walker, p. 179.

69. Fletcher, Ella Adelia (1899). *The Woman Beautiful.* New York: W. M. Young & Co., p. 153.

70. *The Secret Revealed: How to Acquire Personal Beauty* (1889). Chicago: R. S. Peale & Co., p. 31

71. Pallingston, Jessica (1999). Lipstick: A Celebration of the World's Favorite Cosmetic. New York: St. Martin's Press, p. 13.

72. *The Chemists' Annual List* (1870). London: John Sanger & Son, p. 42.

73. Morris, Sir Malcolm Alexander (1883). *The Book of Health.* London: Cassell & Co., p. 896.

74. Leslie, Eliza (1850). *Miss Leslie's Lady's New Receipt-Book: A Useful Guide for Large or Small Families.* Philadelphia: A. Hart, p. 289.

75. *Kendal Mercury* (Cumbria, England), 06 January 1866; p. 2. © British Library Board.

76. Rhind, Jennifer Peace (2014). *Fragrance and Wellbeing.* Philadelphia: Singing Dragon, p. 8.

77. *American Soap Journal and Manufacturing Chemist, Vols. 11-13* (1900). Milwaukee: p. 215.

Index

INDEX